Coaching Reluctant Learners

A Practical Framework for Classroom Success

ENGAGING THE BRAIN & HEART OF TODAY'S STUDENTS

Personalized Strategies, Activities, and Examples to Improve
Middle & High School Student Motivation and Performance

By

Billie Donegan

Dr. Robert K. Greenleaf

Doris Wells-Papanek

Greenleaf & Papanek **Publications**

D1306956

Coaching Reluctant Learners
A Practical Framework for Classroom Success

ENGAGING THE BRAIN & HEART OF TODAY'S STUDENTS
Personalized Strategies, Activities, and Examples to Improve
Middle & High School Student Motivation and Performance

© Copyright 2006 Greenleaf & Papanek **Publications**

First Edition

© 2006 Edited by Sharyn Orvis

Greenleaf & Papanek **Publications**

Contact Information

Dr. Robert K. Greenleaf
P.O. Box 186
Newfield, Maine 04056
207.793.8675 tel.
207.604.0089 cell

bob@greenleaflearning.com
www.greenleaflearning.com

Doris Wells-Papanek
1521 Heritage Court
Lake Forest, Illinois 60045
847.615.9957 tel.
847.615.9958 fax

doris@tailoredlearningtools.com
www.tailoredlearningtools.com

ISBN: 0-9767860-4-4

Dedication

**To the core of public school teachers
who ~ in spite of the odds ~
keep passion and persistence alive.**

Thank you. We need you. Never give up.

OVERVIEW   Key components of this book consist of:

- Introductory Overviews, Key Points, and Summaries
- Strategies, Activities, and Examples
- Research & Results Regarding Major Ideas and Concepts
- Questions for Checking Your Own Classroom Application
- Research Based Resources

KEY POINT

This book is intended to impact educators and learners to:

- **Increase Student Performance by Increasing Student Voice**
  For Previously Disengaged Students to Develop More Ownership of Learning and Set Higher Goals for Themselves

- **Help Teachers Move Toward "Coaches of Learning" Rather than "Deliverers of Content"**
  For Previously "Teacher-Centered" Classrooms to Take More Ownership in "Making" ALL Students Successful

- **Provide a Practical Coaching Framework and Concrete Strategies that Support Instructional Improvement to Close Achievement Gaps**
  For Schools Employing this Coaching Framework to Close Achievement Gaps

TEMPLATES, ORGANIZERS, AND CHARTS

Please feel free to reproduce the templates organizers, and charts in this book for use with your own students.

Also, please take the time necessary to make any adjustments to customize them to the specific demands of the assignments you will provide ~ as well as the learning needs of the students you have in mind. If you are copying any of the templates ~ try enlarging by 110% to adapt them to an 8 1/2 x 11 sheet of paper.

Coaching Reluctant Learners
A Practical Framework for Classroom Success

Table of Contents

Coaching Reluctant Learners

A Practical Framework for Classroom Success

INTRODUCTION

In conversations about student achievement, we will occasionally hear someone say something like, "Well, the problem is teachers don't want to change." Nothing could be farther from the truth. Teachers are AGENTS of change! Everyday in American middle and high schools, teachers are conducting action research: field testing a lesson and figuring out on the drive home after school how to do it better tomorrow, or re-doing the lesson in their mind for this time next year.

Teachers are not afraid of change. They simply know that in the reality of their teaching lives ~ where their plates are overflowing with non-pertinent, non-effective requirements ~ where their rooms are overflowing with non-prepared, non-engaged kids ~ they don't have time for busy work.

As much as they want every child to succeed, they don't have time to read each new book on effective practice that comes out. They are doing their best to read their own new textbooks, content internet resources they've searched out, the set of student papers needing to be graded, and administrative memos.

As much as they worry about why that student in the back isn't "getting it," they don't have time after coming home from their second job or their own child's soccer game to create a differentiated lesson plan for tomorrow that reaches the four learning styles, eight multiple intelligences, and three modalities ~ as well as the two modifications required by the 504!

They DO believe in continuous improvement of their craft. They DO want tools. And they DO realize that what used to work in their classroom sometimes misses the mark with today's kids.

The purpose of this book is to provide *today's* teachers with tools THAT WORK for *today's* students. But even more importantly, this book provides teachers with a condensed version of best practice research in a PRACTICAL FRAMEWORK for classroom success ~ unit-by-unit. We've heard from teachers that have field-tested this design with their own reluctant learners, that it is a *doable* format where both the teacher and the student feel more successful.

Embedded throughout this framework are strategies, activities, and examples that improve student motivation and performance. The goal is to engage the brain and the heart of today's student.

Take a moment to envision a couple of students currently in one of your classes who *are* "reluctant learners." Answer these questions with these students and your classroom in mind.

ENVISION NEED	What skills or attitudes do you want to improve in such students?	What pressures in your classroom are standing in your way?

Now wave a magic wand and step into the future and into the classroom of your dreams.

DREAMING BIG

What would students be doing?
How would they look and feel?
What would they be saying?

What would you be doing?
How would you be different?
How would you look and feel?

Adapted from Greenleaf, "*Creating and Changing Mindsets: Movies of the Mind,*" 2005

How to Use the Book **and the Coaching Framework**

Our job is to provide an easy-to-read, easy-to-follow, step-by-step guide that will provide you with a basic structure for supporting classroom success: six short chapters. Your job is to stick with the sequence, realizing that at the end of the journey you will have mastered a set of key components that fit together to create this success.

Our job is to provide concrete samples of what it looks like in a coaching classroom. Your job is to **try it** in your classroom.

Chapter ONE — What Works with Today's Kids?

The first chapter will introduce you quickly to today's student and the body of research that shows us there are strategies that motivate more students to work harder on more challenging work.

Chapter TWO — Where Do I Find the Time?

Time is a critical component to negotiate in surviving in the high-pressure, high-stakes standardized testing environment. This chapter focuses on the *Doability Factor* and explains how to keep these tools from being "add-ons" to already jam-packed days.

Chapter THREE — Creating a Coaching Framework in the Classroom

This chapter lays out three key segments in any instructional unit that create an environment and structure to support student and teacher success. It will also walk you through a step-by-step process that transforms the traditional classroom into a coaching classroom.

Chapter FOUR — Failure is NOT an Option.

This chapter examines which grading practices *really* reduce non-compliance and "teach" responsibility (grading, homework).

Chapter FIVE — What Do I Need to Make This Work?

This chapter helps you build your own supports, ensuring that the structure and strategies in this book move from the written page into classroom practice.

Chapter SIX — Resources ~ Read More About It...

This chapter provides you with research-based resources that allow you to go deeper into the literature to expand your knowledge and thinking on the topics contained within this book.

**Thanks for adding this tool to your repertoire
and THANK YOU for teaching today's students!**

Chapter **ONE** *What Works* **With Today's Kids?**

"HOW I SPENT MY SUMMER VACATIONS"

Every year at the same time, *the Major* would sequester himself in the basement looking at brochures and maps, and then one evening at dinner he would spring it on us, "This year, we're going to California."

We immediately knew that every minute of our one-week annual vacation had been mapped out, including which historical marker we would stop at and how long between restroom breaks!

At 6:00 a.m. on the appointed day, we would pull out of the driveway. My sister was not allowed to have the music up. My brother was not allowed to read in the car because it made him car sick, which would throw us off schedule. And I was not supposed to ask too many questions.

Within one day, we had learned backseat self-preservation. My head was down working crossword puzzles, my sister was thumbing through *Seventeen*, and my brother was asleep.

Somewhere in New Mexico, I saw an awesome twenty-foot polka-dotted snake on a billboard advertising the **World's Largest Rattle Snake**. "Dad, dad, DAD ~ can we stop?" Noooooo, because then we'd be late for the Fort Union National Monument.

However, my dad was an Army engineer so we spent FOUR HOURS at the Hoover Dam while he explained all the intricacies of how it was built, when it was built, and how many feet of water go over the dam in any one hour. He was loving it! We were hungry. He was ticked we weren't excited; we were mad he wouldn't stop at Las Vegas.

We soon quit looking out the window or bringing up potential stops. We had moved from "Are we there yet?" to "When can we go home?"

One week later we are home on schedule. We covered 2000 miles in one week, yet I remember very little from that trip. I was never sure why he called it a "vacation" because he drove all the way, was exhausted when he got home, and disappointed that we hadn't shared his excitement.

However, 12 months later he had apparently forgotten the experience, because one night at dinner he announced, "This year, we're going to Chicago!"

One of the tough truths about the way we were taught to teach is that it often resembles these summer vacations. We know the destination; we map the route; we plan the stops; we drive; and we pretty much tell students, "Get in the back seat and quit poking your sister!"

Many students wind up acting like captive and passive passengers on a trip they don't want to take. As Kathleen Cushman points out in *Fires in the Bathroom*, "High school becomes something done *to* kids, not *by* kids." (Cushman, 2003)

This book is NOT about letting students get behind the wheel without a license. It is NOT about letting them change the destination. It **IS** about letting them ~ no, **insisting** that they have a voice in the journey.

The goal for Chapter One is to understand that although today's students are getting increasingly harder to teach, there are some common teacher-friendly practices that produce consistent results. **They just may not be the ones we're used to.**

Introducing EMILY AND JASON

The single greatest obstacle to embracing a new classroom design is Emily. She comes on time with her homework done; she sits near the front of the room; she participates in every discussion; and from the excitement on her face you can tell she loves this subject, loves this class, and ~ what the heck ~ loves US.

However, if we look near the back left corner of the room, there sits Jason. Well, there he sits IF he came to class today. He is slumped down in his chair staring at his fingernails with his head bobbing to some internal tune. When we ask where his homework is, we get the highly detailed response of, "Huh?"

The way we were taught to teach works with Emily. We see it every day in every class with multiple students. However, it does NOT work with Jason. We are sometimes tempted to say, "If only Jason would..." or "If only Jason's parents would...," or "If only Jason's middle school teachers had just..."

But let's face it, Jason is here, and every year there are more and more Jasons and fewer and fewer Emilys. If you don't believe me, turn to any colleague who taught twenty-five years ago ~ kids have changed! They are much harder to teach than they used to be, but many of the strategies in our toolbox remain the same ones that brought us widespread success in easier times.

So perhaps this book is a *Jason Survival Guide*: how *you* survive him and *he* survives school. Survive and THRIVE ~ a win/win for both of us!

KEY POINT

Challenging and Challenged

Virtually all teachers want their students to be to be eager thinkers and problem solvers, yet few teachers receive the information and support about how to make that happen in today's environment. Our own sense of powerlessness and frustration increases along with the increase in reluctant learners.

Back in the 1980's, William Glasser saw this oncoming wave of the "challenging and challenged," and urged that a new approach was needed if more students were to work hard in school. He reminded us that "Teaching is a hard job when students make an effort to learn. When they make no effort, it is an impossible one." (Glasser, 1986) Twenty years later, his combination of adolescent psychology and educational theory continues to surface in the research as one of the most effective means of capturing the brains and hearts of today's students:

1. Classrooms where **student voice** is part of the journey.

2. Classrooms where **students do the work of learning and thinking** rather than the teacher.

3. Classrooms that are **learning teams.**

The connection between these statements and success is straight forward:

1. **Increasing student voice and choice increases student motivation and performance.** Reluctant learners don't see where or how their performance, or even their presence at school, makes much of a difference to anyone. Richard Sagor's *Motivating Students and Teachers in an Era of Standards* points out that "When a student feels this way, it is logical for him to wonder why he should bother attending or working hard." (Sagor, 2003)

    Empowering student voice is not equivalent to letting the inmates run the asylum. It's about providing points within any existing unit plan where students not only "get to", but **have to** weigh in. The third of four "foundation mindsets" for student esteem, motivation, and achievement is embedded in an "internal locus of control." This stipulates that youth need to believe they have some influence over outcomes in their lives, if they are to put forth effort. (Greenleaf, 2005)

2. Students need to do more of the working and thinking, and that will only happen if teachers do less of it for them. A colleague once pointed out that we will know we have successful schools when the students go home more tired than the teachers. In the book, *The Learner-Centered Classroom: Strategies for Increasing Student Motivation and Achievement*, it is noted that **long-lasting learning is a constructive process where the learner must be actively engaged in creating his or her own knowledge.** (McCombs, 2001) Conversely, when students are allowed to be passive receptacles or even passive participants, the best teacher-centered lessons will not be optimally effective and will be less likely to reach *all* students.

Activity does not automatically equate to engagement, however. All the numbered-heads together/think-pair-share strategies in the world that keep kids busy and even on task, don't ensure that they are mastering content or even mastering work ethic. It is the highly structured scaffolding and revisiting of "learning about learning" that creates work ethic and *Habits of the Mind.* (Costa & Kallick, 2000)

3. **The whole is stronger than the sum of its parts.** I once had the opportunity to observe a high school teacher in Minneapolis on the first day of school. Budget cuts had resulted in an average class size of 44. Students were crammed into his room with every desk filled, and with seven desks each shared by two students. I watched him count the heads in the room and open with, "Great! There are 41 of you and one of me. Surely, between 42 of us, we can all pass this class!" Here was a teacher who understood you could assess individually yet LEARN TOGETHER. Groups or classes of students who work together will outperform individual achievement (in the aggregate) every time.

RESEARCH ANCHOR

Too many times we mistake activity for accomplishment or as representing mental engagement. Brain research is quite clear ~ the person who does the work (thinking, processing) is the one who does the learning. It is not so much about groups or manipulatives as it is about what is taking place in the learner's mind. "Minds-on" processing that creates memory and recall pathways is the goal of instructional strategies.

Greenleaf, 2005

KEY POINT

Three Philosophical Hurdles

Although brain-based research supports the need for new tools, educational change theory talks about "the incredible gravitational pull of school as usual." We are sometimes surrounded by a culture and colleagues who hold some philosophical assumptions that deter us from trying out new tools for a new kind of student.

If you can clear the **three hurdles** that follow, you have completed your first step to capturing the brains and hearts of today's students.

Hurdle #1 **Understanding Learner Perspectives**

Imagine, if you will, six things that you don't like to do, or that you're not very good at. Perhaps you don't like to balance your checking account or you don't like cleaning the bathroom. Could it even be that you don't like completing lesson plan forms? Maybe you know you struggle with math, or with technology, or with sports. Perhaps you've been told that singing is not your strong suit. Now imagine that each is a class at school and that you have to do those six things every day for 55 minutes. *For many of today's students such a list represents their six period school day.* They arrive at school facing a day full of things they believe they don't like to do, or are not very good at. How would YOU feel? Is it really good news, if your school is on a block schedule and you only have to do four things on your list ~ but you have to do them for 90 minutes!?

The first hurdle is to understand why reluctant learners FEEL the way they do.

Hurdle #2 **Understanding Learner Behaviors**

In workshops, I have frequently given teachers a sixty-second assignment to draw a picture of a person standing at the front of the room. As we complete this exercise, I inevitably see two things happen. There will be one or two people in the room who dash out a stick figure and lay their pencil down in about 7 seconds. There will also be one or two people who can't believe the time is up and want to finish the drawing. As we debrief, the link is always clear and always the same: one set of adults demonstrated some potential talent or previous enjoyment from drawing and were actually wishing they had longer to draw. The other set of adults quickly had an internal dialogue that said, "Can't draw. Why try? Done." 7 seconds flat.

How about you... what would you do?

The second hurdle is to understand why reluctant learners ACT the way they do.

Hurdle #3 **Teacher Efficacy and Empowerment**

Some teachers might say, "I teach math," "I teach history," or "I teach Spanish." Mike Schmoker pointedly and frequently reminds us you can teach to an empty room. Some teachers might say, "I teach children," but in reality we are teaching other people's children in an era where mastery of high level content is critical to their success. What is the single most important common denominator in schools and classrooms that are having success with today's challenging students? It is the teacher's belief that they still have power and potency, and an understanding of their own job description that is much different than the typical response. A teacher who says, "I get whatever students show up in my room to learn math" and "Students leave my room knowing how to speak Spanish, whether they want to or not."

The third, and hardest, hurdle is to believe you have the power and responsibility to reach reluctant learners.

In high-performing/high-results classrooms cited in the 90/90/90 studies or in *Effort and Excellence in Urban Classrooms: Expecting ~ and Getting ~ Success with All Students* (Corbett, Wilson, Williams, 2002), the job description and honest belief is ALL STUDENTS CAN LEARN AND IT'S MY JOB TO SEE THAT THEY DO. Most school mission statements have "all children can learn" embedded in them somewhere, but the actual school conversations have a "but" that is a tip-off that perhaps some staff do not really believe it.

The teachers who are "expecting ~ **and getting** ~ success with all students," believe you can't say you teach math until the kids leave the room knowing math. They understand how brave it is to be a teacher with that job description, because while your colleague might have an easy job with her third period class, your third period might be a challenge (to say the least). And regardless of which third period, they *still* believe their job description hasn't changed.

Research & RESULTS

Brain Sciences and Learning

We must shift our thinking and our strategies about classroom management and organization to reflect what we now know about how the adolescent brain responds to its environment and situation. Throughout this book we will synthesize information and ideas from a wide variety of people and sources that have connected neuroscience to educational practice.

Primary research articles and statistical studies of "what works" are not easy reading. Still, it is critical to become aware of the best practices that have shown to increase classroom success with more students. We will occasionally point out what the Department of Education calls "scientifically-based research" and proven best practices from such researchers as Bob Marzano, Mike Schmoker, Rick DuFour, Thomas Guskey, Katie Haycock, Charlotte Danielson, Rick Stiggins, Doug Reeves, and others.

Effective Practices   We know practices such as those listed below have been studied and shown to increase and sustain student learning outcomes:

- Focus: Identifying specific, targeted student learning outcomes

- Collaboration: Teachers working together to score student work relative to common assessment

- Frequent (daily/weekly) formative assessment/feedback and reporting of student progress

- Regular non-fiction writing across the disciplines

- Safe environments in which to explore, communicate, and test learning ideas

- Student engagement with compare/contrast and similar different strategies

- Bi-modal representations that include both verbal and visual elements, linked together in "packets," to sustain memory and significantly increase recall.

Effective Processing for Long-term Memory Depends on Certain Activities

1. **STRENGTH** ~ Memory records are assumed to have "strength," which increases with repeated practice ~ four exposures in no more than two days apart

2. **DEPTH OF PROCESSING** ~ Identify characteristics of topic or subtopics, or provide and explore detail

3. **ELABORATION** ~ Variety of associations made with information, or making varied connections.

What Today's Kids Need

Greenleaf: 1991, 2005

The Four Foundation Mindsets
Creating and Changing Mindsets of Today's Youth.

If we are to co-construct productive attitudes that embrace learning, the origins of learner motivation are integral to our and their success in the classroom. Constructs of internal dialogue, locus of control, efficacy, and mentorship permeate the literature regarding student success. The National School Improvement Project condensed the field and further framing comes from the book, "Creating and Changing Mindsets." Four foundational mindset categories that under gird esteem, achievement, and motivation are identified across the literature as:

1. **I Am Capable ~ How the learner perceives him/herself.**
   Am I capable of doing this? If I feel capable, I act capable. If I feel unworthy, I act unworthy.

2. **Today Connects With Tomorrow ~ Empowerment to find motivation.**
   How will the efforts I am investing today connect with desired outcomes in my tomorrows?

3. **I Make A Difference ~ Empowerment for being a respected player.**
   Do I have a say, can I impact potential outcomes? Do you respect and believe in me?

4. **Someone Believes In Me ~ Pays Attention to Me.**
   If I struggle or even fail, will it matter to anyone else? Is it safe to try? Will anyone notice if I do... or don't? Will your expectations stay consistently high... or convey that you don't believe I can do this?

The literature ~ and our daily interactions with students guide us: "When we [students]... have few or none [of the foundation mindsets]... we become more negative and pessimistic about possibilities We expend time and energy in resisting and avoiding [tasks at hand]."

Assessment

Stiggins and Chappius, 2006

"No Child Left Behind has lit an assessment fire in our nation. Off-the-shelf assessments may be marketed as 'formative assessments,' but they don't help teachers understand or apply the strategies that have been proven to increase student learning. They do not show teachers how to make learning targets clear to students, or how to help students differentiate between strong and weak work. They do not help teachers understand what kinds of feedback are most effective, or how to find the time to provide that feedback. They do not help teachers show students how to assess their own strengths and weaknesses, nor do they emphasize the motivational power of having students track and share their learning."

IN SUMMARY   In his article, *Defy the 'Knowing-Doing Gap,'* Doug Reeves examines the latest research and states frankly, "One of the greatest frustrations in education is that success is really not a mystery. There is a significant body of research that suggests that certain replicable strategies in teaching have a high probability of success. Therefore, the greatest challenge is not necessarily in knowing what to do, but how to do it and, more commonly, how to persuade colleagues to use effective strategies." (Reeves, 2002)

Our job will be to show you what those strategies look like in your classroom so that, after you've tried them, you can share your success with colleagues.

READ MORE ABOUT IT...   Chapter Six will provide additional information on such studies and programs as the Center for Performance Assessment, National Student Aspirations Project, and other resources ~ should you want to dig deeper into the literature or explore resources further than can be accommodated in this book.

Chapter ONE *Checklist for Success*

☐ Do I feel the need or the desire to be even more successful?

☐ Am I looking for tools that work with today's students?

☐ Am I willing to risk trying new tools, knowing that trying things for the first time is always bumpy?

☐ Can I empathize ~ or at least cope with ~ the way reluctant learners feel and act in my class, and use that information to connect with the students in a less adversarial way?

☐ Am I willing to increase student voice and student responsibility for the work of learning, even if it seems easier just to do it for them?

☐ Knowing it would be much easier to abdicate responsibility to the ever handy scapegoats of student motivation and home environment, do I want to become a "no excuses" teacher?

The influx of more challenging students should convince us we need new tools. The research shows us effective tools are out there. We are willing and eager... **if we just had time.**

Chapter **TWO** *Where Do I* **Find the Time?**

OVERVIEW

Having taught for 28 years in the same high school, I outlived nine principals, six superintendents, and Ross Perot being in charge of Texas education. During my time there, two opposing forces converged: the growth of the standards/benchmarks movement, and Texas mandating students pass the state assessment to graduate.

In the meantime, many well-intentioned initiatives came... and went. Although all were aimed at increasing student achievement, most wound up resembling activity more than accomplishment.

- Vision statements were composed and grids filled in ~ complete with measurable goals, action steps, and timelines. The strategic plan was posted on the web and the mission statement hung on the wall. Test scores remained the same.

- The district office spent countless hours and dollars in a highly complicated vertical and horizontal alignment and distributed a vast document to every school. Test scores remained the same.

- Pacing guides were constructed for core curricula to make sure no benchmark subset went uncovered. Test scores remained the same.

- Principals required lesson plans documenting that today's lesson was addressing "17.3.b" and teachers religiously ~ or fictionally ~ transcribed them into lesson plan books and on the board. Test scores remained the same.

- Consultants arrived from out of state to ensure us that *cooperative learning,* or *differentiated instruction,* or *quilt questioning,* or *learning styles,* or *behavior interventions,* or *silent sustained reading* would – at last ~ raise test scores. You guessed it, test scores remained the same.

There were not only good intentions behind the above "solutions," there is also solid research. The missing ingredient was TIME. Without an understanding of **power standard teaching** and an **in-class coaching framework** to support the integration of these practices into the reality of a teacher's life, even the best practices will never reach most classrooms.

Chapter Two will verify what good teachers already know: high-speed coverage of standards and benchmarks is not a formula for success. Teaching what matters most to depth and complexity, in ways that involve all students, is.

The road has narrowed and the speed has increased, while authentic learning and passionate teaching is being jettisoned like litter… and we do not even acknowledge how far we've veered off course. Schools obsess about how "drop out rates" impact their State Report Card, yet fail to acknowledge the growing amount of students ~ including many at the top ~ who have dropped out mentally and emotionally.

KEY POINT

Power Standards

Most teachers agree we should hold students to high standards. Most teachers agree that every classroom should exhibit a consistency of standards so that students are ensured a good education in the subject regardless of which teacher they get. Most teachers even agree that we should be held accountable for seeing that certain standard content knowledge and skills are taught in each discipline. It is not the word "standard" that frightens and frustrates us. It is the overwhelming amount of them! And researchers concur:

Larry Ainsworth   If we covered every standard and benchmark just once, and never revisited it again, we would have to keep kids in school K-22.

Doug Reeves   It is clear to most teachers who lack a 400-day school year and pupils with photographic memories, that there are simply too many standards.

Bob Marzano   The main problem with standards is that we put history teachers in a room together to write the history standards… and they did so with gluttonous abandonment.

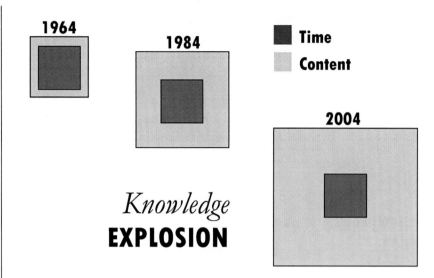

Knowledge
EXPLOSION

Dr. Michael White, in *Why We Hate Standards,* put forth that when standards were introduced, we never stopped teaching what we had already been teaching. (White, 2002) We tried to add standards to the school day and to our workload. Big mistake! Most research shows that American teachers are already trying to cover too much material. In Singapore, it's against the law to adopt a textbook with more than 100 pages. Compare that to America where the educational mantra is still "finish the book." And the bigger the book, the better. Fourth grade teachers in Japan are content to cover 17 math topics. And they have 250 days of school in which to do it. By comparison, fourth grade teachers in the U.S. scurry to cover on average, 78 topics in a 180-day school year.

RESEARCH ANCHOR

"When there is too much to do, improvement becomes disjointed and incoherent... system overload may be the biggest threat to genuine improvement."

Schmoker, 2003

In forty years, the time students spend in school has remained constant, but the content we are asked to cover has exploded. In striving to "cover" everything, teachers readily admit to a fast-paced, shallower approach to course content than they want. **Teachers need to give themselves permission to accurately interpret the perceived district or state message, "You better cover it all," into the more accurate translation, "Test scores better go up."**

Educational research has been screaming at us that higher test scores have absolutely no correlation to how much gets covered, but *everything* to do with how much <u>gets remembered</u> when the assessments roll around. With the obsessive focus on state assessments that includes everything from "test question of the day" to pep rallies prior to the state test, schools have lost site of the fact that we can focus on quality teaching and learning ~ without ever mentioning the state test ~ AND TEST SCORES WILL GO UP.

The question is not whether or not I [we] have time to cover the material. The question is whether or not the students have sufficient time and opportunity to learn the material... and to learn it well.

KEY POINT

Power Standard Teaching

Power Standard Teaching is a paradigm shift from **ALL content** and some kids to **ALL kids** on *some* content.

Instead of SOME of the Students, Knowing the Content...

ALL Students CAN and WILL Learn What Matters the Most.

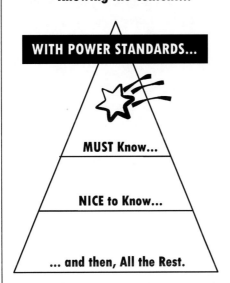

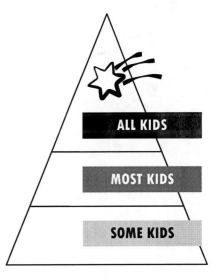

Allowing our classroom to move from covering it all and losing some students, to covering some but getting ALL students to mastery on it, carries with it two important responsibilities.

The **first responsibility** is in agreeing that the material we choose to get ALL students to learn will be the "must knows." All standards are NOT equal. The simple truth is that within any state document, within any district curriculum guide, within any course scope and sequence, and *within any course unit and textbook chapter*, SOME STANDARDS ARE MORE IMPORTANT THAN OTHERS IN TERMS OF OVERALL STUDENT SUCCESS.

The Center for Performance Assessment describes identifying Power Standards as "A systematic and balanced approach to distinguishing the standards that are absolutely essential for student success from those that are 'nice to know'." (Reeves, 2004) In reality, it can be as simple as two teachers opening up to Chapter 27 and asking themselves, "What lies within this chapter that is worth remembering and using ten years from now?" We guarantee you that their answer can be back-walked to a state standard by the district office, without their ever having to spend hours parsing the state and district documents.

The **second responsibility** is in teaching the Power Standards we have selected to ALL students and to depth and complexity ~ increasing both rigor and relevance.

Three key elements are essential as we work with students to master power standards. They are Rigor, Relevance, Relationships ~ because it is those three that lead us to Retention.

RIGOR, *Relevance, Relationships... leading to Retention*

Rigor is not just for the "honors kids." It must be and **can be** applied to ALL ~ IF we embrace **quality** over *quantity*. Kati Haycock of EdTrust constantly reminds us that kids can only become as capable as what they are asked to do. By identifying less ~ but essential ~ material within the chapter we are teaching, we now have the time to "take it up a level" in both assignments and assessments.

It can be as simple as examining questions and activities to see where they are on the good ole Bloom's Taxonomy. In describing the increasingly complex ways in which we think, we know the low end involves acquiring knowledge and being able to recall or locate that knowledge. The high end represents complex ways in which individuals use knowledge, such as taking several pieces of knowledge and combining them in both logical and creative ways. The question we have to ask ourselves is, "How often do we give assignments and assessment questions on the higher end?" **Like the following examples,** in power standards teaching, assignments and assessments may "cover less" but ASK MORE.

EXAMPLE	**From...**	**To...**
10th Grade Writing Assignment	Write a composition of at least 4 paragraphs on Martin Luther King's most important contribution to society. Illustrate your work with a neat cover page. Neatness counts.	A frequent theme in literature is the conflict between the individual and society. From literature you have read, select a character who struggled with society. In a well-developed essay, identify the character and explain why this character's conflict with society is important. What attribute did the character possess that you would find most useful in your own personal struggles?
Source	www.edtrust.org	

EXAMPLE	**From...**	**To...**
Science Assignment	In which part of a cell does the Calvin Cycle take place? a. in the stroma in chloroplasts b. in the microfilaments of the cytoskeleton c. in the membranes of the endoplasmic reticulum d. in the vacuoles of the animal cells	In teams of two, think of a way in which the term "fixation" is used by people you know. Create a definition from that common usage. NOW, describe how that definition could possibly apply to *carbon fixation.* What might "three stages" of ***personal* fixation reactions** look like? How do they parallel our text? In BOTH cases, how can *fixation* become a cycle?
Source	www.nst.gov	

Let's face it. We'd have to give up some content from the photosynthesis unit in biology in order to coach students to think and work through the second example and, besides, we couldn't use a Scantron. But should a question over Calvin-Benson come up on the state exam in March of the following year, the chances of students being able to access long-term memory to retrieve needed information have a much better likelihood.

Science teachers would know better than us if the Calvin-Benson Cycle is a power standard in biology. The "power" in **power standard teaching** is in the individual teacher's reflection or in collegial conversations to determine *which* concepts in a chapter/unit deserve delving into with more depth and complexity, and how we might do it.

The key is to understand that, as teachers, RIGOR means higher quality and deeper thinking. As coaches, it is setting up supports where students of all levels have the ability to deepen their thinking and improve the quality of their work.

KEY POINT

Rigor, **RELEVANCE***, Relationships... leading to Retention*

There is no dichotomy between increasing academic rigor in the classroom and making education relevant to students. Relevance is directly related to a student's understanding of how learning can be applied to life outside school. Increasing relevance can range from simply telling students how a concept *could* be related, to challenging students to actually apply the learning to an authentic, unpredictable, real-world problem.

One need only read Schmoker's, *The Crayola Curriculum*, to realize quickly that many well-intentioned efforts at relevance ~ making content videos, translating content into rap lyrics, and content projects ~ may take time and keep kids "engaged" yet remain at the low end of application.

Bill Daggett's September 2005 white paper, *Achieving Academic Excellence through Rigor and Relevance*, points out that if a teacher has high rigor in assignments and assessments but a low-level of application, the learning has still not been maximized. Likewise, relevance also has a quality continuum.

We need their brains engaged as well as their bodies. It is in highly rigorous and highly relevant application that students develop skills such as inquiry, investigation, and experimentation. Daggett has added an Application Model to measure, along with Bloom's, and created a clear visual that helps teachers identify the level of rigor and relevance contained in an assignment or assessment.

Daggett's Application Model

If Bloom's Taxonomy is about the level of *thinking*, Daggett's Application Model is about the level of *action*: **putting knowledge to use.** The low end of this continuum is knowledge acquired for its own sake, while the high end requires use of that knowledge to solve complex problems and to create unique projects, designs, and other work products for use in unpredictable real-world situations.

Bloom's **Taxonomy**   *Daggett's* **Quadrants**

Bloom's Taxonomy	Daggett's Quadrants	
Evaluation 6 Synthesis 5 Analysis 4	**C** *Assimilation* Students extend and refine acquired knowledge to be able to use that knowledge automatically and routinely to analyze and solve complex problems and create unique solutions.	**D** *Adaptation* Students have the competence to think in complex ways and to apply knowledge and skills they have acquired. Even when confronted with perplexing unknowns, students are able to create solutions and take action that further develops skills and knowledge.
Application 3 Understanding 2 Awareness 1	**A** *Acquisition* Students gather and store bits of information. Students are primarily expected to remember or understand knowledge.	**B** *Application* Students use acquired knowledge to solve problems, design solutions, and complete work.

Daggett's **Continuum**

1	2	3	4	5
Knowledge	Apply in Discipline	Apply Across Disciplines	Apply to Predictable Real-World Situations	Apply to Unpredictable Real-World Situations

The International Center for Leadership in Education
www.daggett.com

In power standard teaching, we approach each unit with confidence that depth over breadth will get us better results. In *Trivial Pursuits*, Wolk states, "The slavish commitment to coverage results in facts and information being valued more than reasoning and understanding. It has prompted schools to isolate bits of knowledge rather than connect them in interdisciplinary ways. And knowledge out of context is trivia."

To move from teaching to learning, we must "... help students make the connections between ideas and concepts... help them see the relationships between knowledge within and across disciplines... give them the opportunity to apply what they learn in school to their daily lives. If that were to occur, perhaps more of them would not only know it for the test, they would know how to go on learning for a lifetime." (Wolk, 2003)

KEY POINT

Rigor, Relevance, **RELATIONSHIPS**... *leading to Retention*

When Bill Gates spoke to state governors in 2005 at the National Summit on High School Education, he referred to what many have called the new 3Rs, noting that "The third R is Relationships ~ making sure kids have a number of adults who know them, look out for them, and **push them** to achieve." Glasser pointedly remarks that "Trying the old survival society threat of telling them to buckle down because they needed school for later security fell on deaf ears." (Glasser, 1986) Yet these same students do "listen" and work hard for adults for whom they care strongly. The power of relationships is in leveraging how students feel about school and about teachers, into how they perform and how they are *willing to push themselves.*

Any number of advocates of the smaller learning communities' movement recognize that "kids don't care how much they learn until they learn how much you care." The *Institute for Research and Reform in Education* notes an emerging consensus exists in the research that "...relationships matter, and are linked to student engagement and achievement." Boynton and Boynton cite the building of teacher-student relationships as the foremost step in preventing and solving discipline problems, as well as creating the climate where students will be more wiling to learn. (Boynton & Boynton, 2005)

When students enter a classroom where peer relationships, as well as the relationship with the teacher, support and promote academic risk-taking and working together as a team, reluctant learners begin to come into the fold.

Alfie Kohn states, "It's about the real respect we show by asking all students what they think about how things are going, and how we might do things differently ~ not the selective reinforcement we offer to some students when they please us." (Kohn, 2005)

When students know that the teacher believes they are capable of more and cares enough about them to refuse to accept less, a bond will forge that takes learning to the third power.

The Power of **the 3Rs**

It is the power of these "3Rs," combined and actualized inside the classroom that captures the brains and hearts of today's students.

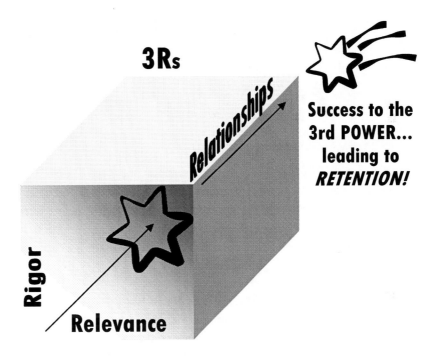

Creating a classroom where every unit focuses on the Power Standards within that unit allows us the time <u>to work WITH students during class</u> on the important work of learning, to master what matters most.

- We then have the time to **work with kids** to set high expectations, and align assessments and teaching, to help ALL of them meet those expectations. Even more importantly, it gives us time to talk about the learning process so that students learn to think, construct, and retain information. This is the learning power of **Rigor.**

- We then have the time to **work with kids** to create innovative and engaging options to keep them motivated, wrapping academic content and skills in contexts that have meaning for students. This is the learning power of **Relevance.**

- We then have the time to build "team" in the classroom, creating an environment that is friendly, focused, and supportive of learning risks. We are building a community of learning where students are known, cared for, and accountable, and where students and the teacher collaborate with one another rather than operate in isolation. This is the learning power of **Relationships.**

**Brain-based research shows that a
fourth "R" will then follow... *RETENTION*.**

Research & RESULTS

Retention

Brain and Expectation

Brain sciences strongly support the basis of an expectation of rigor (expectations of competence), relevance (personally worth doing), and relationships (in a safe environment) as crucial elements to learning ~ learning that "gets it in" our head ~ and importantly ~ "gets it back out" later on. Lowered expectations diminish motivation to do the initial processing required for sustained memory.

Brain and Episodic Memory

Gordon, 2005

Episodic memory, largely active with dates, names, and general information ~ is the primary domain of content knowledge ~ and is often a fragile memory formation. Without substantial effort and frequent reinforcement, connections and pathways tend to "dissolve" resulting in what is referred to as knowledge decay (forgetting). Though some learners are quite adept at acquiring massive amounts of information quickly (to their credit!), this does not always transfer into long-term memory.

Brain and Procedural Memory

Brain and procedural memory is involved with process, imagery, and the ongoing relationship of ideas. It builds more lasting connections through concepts, context, emotion (personal meaning), and bimodal (visual/verbal) constructs. Once formed, it has a longer "shelf-life," far more resistant to demise and as much as 50% more accessible for recall.

Brain and Motivation

National Center for Student Aspirations, 2005

The *National Center for Student Aspirations* has conducted a recent review of the literature that anchors rigor, relevance, and relationships ~ toward greater retention. Their findings suggest that there are three constructs required by learners today. They are:

1. Social Supports
Emotional support, guidance, and recognition through caring relationships

2. Intrinsic Motivation
The internal desire to attain goals, enhanced through voice, that influences the journey along the way ~ building persistence and commitment

3. Self-Efficacy
One's belief in one's ability to accomplish things ~ a level of confidence ~ attributing success and/or failure to effort rather than ability.

IN SUMMARY

Thus, all of our interests in: teaching for deeper understanding; strategizing across Daggett's Application Model; applying Bloom's Taxonomy; using the National Center for Student Aspiration's constructs for aspirations; and creating an environment that builds the four foundation mindsets of esteem, motivation, and achievement ~ are all viable toward sustaining learner... and learning outcomes. Cover less, know more.

If you have any doubts about what brain research suggests regarding retention, try several self-checks on behalf of your school. Give a classroom of seniors the ninth grade end of course Biology or World Geography exam. You may discover that even students who made B's and A's in those courses are no longer capable of passing. That "rigorous" colleague who insisted he couldn't slow down because he was preparing them for college, might want to warn the colleges that his students may know how to cram, but they haven't retained much of the content to take with them into college courses. You can even test yourself by giving your students the identical test they took two months ago. Which parts did they remember and which parts did they forget? And WHY?

Learning, in the end, is about LEARNER attempts to learn, more than about teacher attempts to teach.

READ MORE ABOUT IT...

We encourage you to read more about what noted authors offer in Chapter Six: "Resources ~ Read More About It..."

Now it's time to create a classroom structure and culture where we as teachers, and our students, both believe "If it's worth asking, it's worth remembering."

Chapter TWO *Checklist for Success*

☐ Do you feel like you are being asked to move too fast or cover too much?

☐ Are you ready to move from coverage mode to a focus on Power Standards within each unit or chapter? (Knowing you may have to prove to colleagues that your students will be getting a better education.)

☐ Will you be willing to let go of some material ~ and maybe even some "fun" lessons that keep kids entertained ~ in order to focus on the MUST KNOW's within that chapter?

☐ Are you confident that you could recognize high-level rigor and high-level relevance when you examine assignments or assessments?

☐ Do you believe getting kids to do quality work is more important than the quantity of assignments turned in?

☐ Could you fully engage in being a "no excuses" teacher in a way that students understand as a demonstration of how much you care about their success?

☐ Are you willing to talk to and with kids about what rigor, relevance, and relationships "look like" in a classroom?

We are willing and eager; we will carve out time WITHIN our class period by focusing on Power Standards... **but will ALL students participate?**

Chapter **THREE** *Creating a Coaching* **Classroom Framework**

COACHING MINDSETS

"There are teachers with a rare ability to enter a child's mind; it's as if their ability to get there at all gives them the right to stay forever." Such a turning point came in Michael Lewis' life when he was fourteen years old. The person who entered his mind was the irascible and sometimes terrifying Coach Fitz, who put the ball in his hand with the game on the line "… and managed to convey such confident trust in my ability that I had no choice but to live up to it." So begins *Coach: Lessons on the Game of Life* by Michael Lewis, author of *Moneyball* and *Liar's Poker*. Almost every teacher I talk with has an influential teacher in their past that they will remember "forever." For a surprising number, that teacher was often a coach ~ in fact or in actions.

I admit to being a sports fan all my life: pro baseball in October, the March Madness of college basketball, and Texas high school football on Friday nights. All seemed to carry the magic of dreaming big, performing above expectations, sticking together/winning together. Yet it was the victories of underdogs and the role of the coach in those victories that seemed to connect with me the most.

I knew coaching was not about being a friend, and maybe not even about being a mentor. It was about knowing how to spot potential; knowing how to build teamwork and how to build confidence; knowing how to train and when to push the limits. It was about knowing how to get the most out of the individual by getting the most out of the team. It was about knowing how to make adjustments in the game to snatch victory from the jaws of defeat. Never be afraid of the last two minutes. Most importantly, it was about *really, really* wanting to win… for them.

I'm certainly not the first to see how easily this metaphor translates to other areas. Jim Collins talks about coaching in *Good to Great,* and countless authors have provided insight into how coaching works to raise achievement ~ in business, in your personal life, and most recently, in education.

COACHING APPROACHES

When I first read Thomas Crane's, *The Heart of Transformational Coaching: Using Coaching to Create a High-Performance Culture*, it was for use in my work with principals, not students. Yet with every chapter I read, I knew that what we hunger for as teachers is a framework for establishing a high-performance culture in our classroom. I also realized that the most powerful role for a teacher in the classroom was as a transformational COACH. Every teacher has it in them.

You can take a team with less talent and less money and still win the game. You can lose a game and still win the series. It is not about style, but about substance. You can be a polished, articulate Tom Landry or a gregarious, gruff Vince Lombardi and still get the job done.

Likewise, moving from teacher-to-coach in the classroom doesn't mean you have to change your *style*, but it does mean you have to change your *role*. Richard Sagor believes teachers can meet the challenge the standards movement calls for, "... but to do so requires a major change in the prevailing student-teacher relationship. Fortunately, a prototype relationship exists within the school environment... In extracurricular activities such as music, drama, and athletics, the adult-student relationship is based on a very different premise."

Some coaches and some teams win with regularity: Red Auerbach (Boston Celtics), Don Shula (Miami Dolphins), Pat Summitt (Tennessee Volunteers). Different venues, different styles, same formula: *hard work works*. **And it is a COACHING FRAMEWORK that provides the scaffolding to produce hard work from *all* players.**

Perhaps the best book ever written about teaching is *They Call Me Coach*. For 27 years, John Wooden led the UCLA basketball team to unsurpassed records. They won ten NCAA national championships ~ seven in a row. ESPN voted him the Coach of the Century, yet Wooden himself says it was not his style or his talent, but his STRUCTURE that built success. Structure provides winning coaches the opportunity to synthesize the varying degrees of talent in the locker room into a predictable winning team. The *Pyramid of Success* that led to the Bruin dynasty was a framework that supported players in becoming the best they are capable of becoming.

The goal of Chapter Three is to provide teachers with a coaching framework *within their own classroom.* There are three simple pieces and eight specific steps that will create your own pyramid of success with the players you have in the room. Our classroom goal is to move from an environment where students ~ and sometimes the teacher ~ "play the school game" to an environment where students are engaged in the exciting, challenging, *joyous* game of learning.

The Coaching Framework in a "Nutshell"

THE METAPHOR FOR THE FRAMEWORK

In the coaching framework we create for our classroom, think of the semester course as your season, and each unit as a game in that season. The opponent lies inside the book ~ challenging material worth facing and conquering. Like it or not, the team you bring to the field to face the opponent sits in front of you. It is what you do TOGETHER that determines whether all of you approach this challenge as a chore, or as an adventure. On page 131, we offer two additional metaphors (music and classroom teaching) to provide clarity about the "coaching/football" metaphor referenced throughout this book.

The three key pieces in a coaching framework are: Pre-Game Preparation, Half-Time (On-the-Field and In-the-Game), and the Post-Game Reflections. **Even if you do not change a single minute of your unit lesson from the way it looked last year** ~ yet embed a pre-game activity, a half-time activity, and a post-game activity ~ more students will get on the field to work harder, better and faster. Chances of victory will go up.

Admittedly, there will be sports terms used in our illustration that will ~ if you don't already use them ~ give you more cachét with the field-house crew. Each term used has a direct and clear relationship to creating a concrete picture of what this looks like, and **how it works**, to create a classroom where more students work harder on more challenging material to accomplish authentic, and lasting learning.

OVERVIEW   **The Coaching Framework @ a Glance**

It is a practical coaching framework that Emily will quickly learn to love, and ~ even better ~ that will get Jason to look up and take notice. Brain-based research suggests that, for maximum learning to take place, every piece of knowledge should be experienced through a process called:

Brief ⇨ Meta-cognition ⇨ Debrief

For our purposes, let's imagine it's Monday night... so we'll call it:

Pre-Game ⇨ Half-time ⇨ Post-Game

Are you ready for some football?

Pre-Game Preparation

SETTING THE STAGE
FOR SUCCESS IN THE
COACHING CLASSROOM

In an era of pacing guides and common assessments, it often seems that the most expedient scenario in the classroom is to point out to students, "I've only got 15 days to cover this unit, open up to page 124." We have miles to go before we sleep. It's the cross-country vacation trip all over again. We pull out of the educational driveway not even leaving time for kids to grab their backpack before getting into the car. They're quickly shuffled into the back seat and the car starts moving, but they are *not* ready for the trip.

What if ~ within the same timeframe ~ we determined that we are covering fewer miles but taking more important stops? That would allow us time *before* leaving the driveway to determine the most important destinations. Thus, Power Standard teaching!

Every coach knows that what you do PRIOR to getting on the field matters most. One of the first things to notice when watching teams prepare for the game is that the players leave at the end of each practice much more tired than the coach.

Our goal is to have that same level of intellectual exhaustion happen inside our classrooms. Just as there is something fulfilling after a tiring workout, that same fulfillment and "workout" should occur in the classroom. It can't happen if **we** continue to do all the preparation and work for them.

Normally, well-intentioned teachers hand students the chapter expectations, assignments, due dates, and rubrics each time they enter into a new unit. Many have stayed up late into the night designing ways to "grab their attention" and to make clear what the key objectives are going to be and why what is being learned is important. And, of course, Emily is listening.

In *Telling Stories of Change*, McCombs states, "Probably the scariest change for me is that I work right along with students now instead of for them... I'm somewhat embarrassed to admit it now, but I frequently came back from the summer with everything done for the first semester and I hadn't met one single student yet."

In each step of PRE-GAME activities, we are going to look for ways that this same preparation would happen **inside our classrooms *with* our students.** *Students* will be doing the thinking and working, <u>coached by us to perform at their best</u>.

Instead of doing the pre-game work ourselves and then "telling" our students, we are going to begin with **coaching "conversations."** The way in which we hold those conversations will depend on our personal teaching style: the goal is simply for students to have a voice ~ whether they want to or not.

- Teachers who prefer a quiet and tightly controlled classroom may choose to have students heard through short journaling or written survey conversations.

- Teachers skilled in cooperative learning may choose to have students work in small teams and then hear from each team.

- Teachers who like to juggle multiple voices in a larger venue may choose the give and take of a whole "out-loud" classroom conversation.

It matters not in which style these conversations are held ~ it matters GREATLY that the ARE held.

In our coaching framework, PRE-GAME PREPARATION contains:

Step ONE ~ *Scouting for Power Standards*

Let's look at the coaching metaphor through the eyes of two teachers with the responsibility of getting through one of their units in just fifteen days. One teacher will take the risk of "coaching" during those fifteen days, while the other will stick to school as usual.

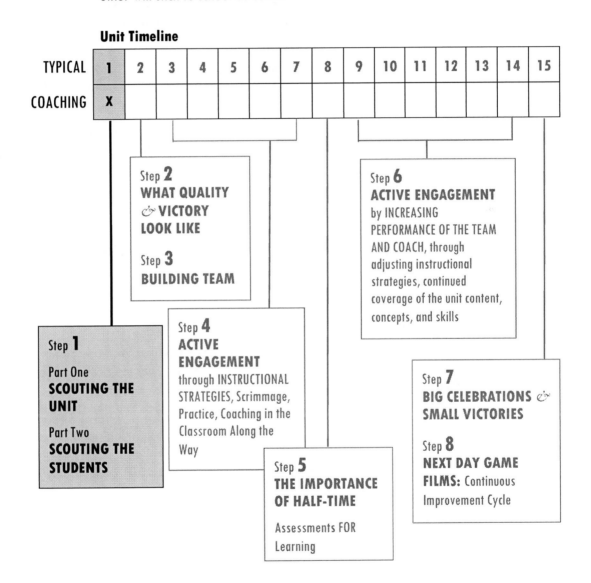

Unit Timeline

	1	2	3	4	5	6	7	8	9	10	11	12	13	14	15
TYPICAL	1	2	3	4	5	6	7	8	9	10	11	12	13	14	15
COACHING	X														

Step **2**
WHAT QUALITY
& **VICTORY**
LOOK LIKE

Step **3**
BUILDING TEAM

Step **6**
ACTIVE ENGAGEMENT
by INCREASING
PERFORMANCE OF THE TEAM
AND COACH, through
adjusting instructional
strategies, continued
coverage of the unit content,
concepts, and skills

Step **1**
Part One
**SCOUTING THE
UNIT**
Part Two
**SCOUTING THE
STUDENTS**

Step **4**
**ACTIVE
ENGAGEMENT**
through INSTRUCTIONAL
STRATEGIES, Scrimmage,
Practice, Coaching in the
Classroom Along the
Way

Step **7**
BIG CELEBRATIONS *&*
SMALL VICTORIES

Step **8**
**NEXT DAY GAME
FILMS:** Continuous
Improvement Cycle

Step **5**
**THE IMPORTANCE
OF HALF-TIME**

Assessments FOR
Learning

KEY POINT

Scouting the Unit

In the classroom, we sometimes work too hard to "convince" kids that what they are learning is important. Our role as a coach is to involve students in scouting for importance themselves, in order to build their own belief in the mission. In sports, a crucial step in scouting is to make sure that the players understand the opponent. Coaches ask their players to watch tapes so that they clearly know the answer ahead of time to "What are we up against?"

In order to have time for scouting in the classroom, you must be a power standards teacher. You know from the onset that you will be focusing on the "must knows" within the chapter, and letting go of some other chapter content in order to free time to involve students in deeper thinking and more complex work.

Tom Kohl, an Ohio volleyball coach, counsels his girls that "Performing your best requires smarts. The battle is often won long before the play begins in the knowledge you acquire about your opponent... That knowledge is often overlooked, but can definitely provide you a decisive edge. Prior to any competition, you should scout your opponent's play if possible."

In a classroom, we can either *tell* students what the important pieces of the chapter are and how we should tackle the mastery of this chapter, or we can ask *them* to "scout" the chapter ~ looking for key points and terms that will become the power standards the team will need to know in order to "win" (conquer the materials).

Get ready. Doing the work for them is much easier than coaching them to do it themselves. They have been conditioned over the previous years of school to be passive passengers. The first time you ask them to think, to discern, to decide, to rate, to rank ~ they will look at you like deer in the headlights.

Jason is likely to grumble, "That's why *you're* getting paid." Take a deep, calming breath, and reply, "I promise to earn my money; but I'm going to do it by getting YOU to where I know you can be as a thinker and a _____ (scientist, reader, historian, wide receiver)."

WE WANT TO ACCOMPLISH TWO GOALS IN <u>SCOUTING THE UNIT</u> *WITH* KIDS:

1. Identify the **must knows** within the chapter and "let go" of other content that is not as crucial to life-long learning. This will send a clear message to students in the room, "We are not going to waste our time on extraneous knowledge or 'busy work,' but will only concentrate on what is critical to YOU."

2. Involve students in a **sense of ownership** in what those "must knows" are by having them engage in a foreshadowing of what will be important to master. As the coach, your job becomes making sure the power standards get identified. I once had a teacher tell me, "95% of what I intended to do was identified by the kids, but now they think it's their idea. The other 5% was actually stuff I *wish* I'd thought of!"

Although you as the teacher are the ultimate authority on which of the POWER STANDARDS for each unit becomes the targeted mission for the class, after that determination it is important that you allow students input in designing how to achieve mastery. Students should be involved in designing the plans for activities, assessments, and connections. They should be allowed a choice in determining learning modes that fit their needs and interests. They should be given a voice in the selection of groups, selection of homework approach, and selection of support opportunities.

PLEASE notice that NOWHERE does it say a student may opt out of doing homework, working in a group, getting the needed support, getting assessed, or mastering the material. It simply says that by providing students choices in the "hows" of the approach, they will be much more agreeable and productive in mastering the "whats."

RESEARCH ANCHOR

Foundation Mindset #2 ~ "The efforts I am investing today are connected to the outcomes I hope to have happen in my tomorrows. I must believe that given reasonable effort...a desired outcome can happen."

Greenleaf, "*Creating and Changing Mindsets*:" 1991, 2005

RESEARCH ANCHOR

"...student voice activities can create meaningful experiences for youth that help to meet fundamental developmental needs ~ especially for students who otherwise do not find meaning in their school experiences. Specifically, this research finds a marked consistency in the growth of agency, belonging and competence ~ three assets that are central to youth development."

Mitra, 2004

STRATEGIES for Scouting the Unit WITH Kids

IDENTIFYING PRIORITIES

The content and context of your unit materials may determine the way in which you involve students in scouting for power standards. However, here a few examples of what could be done with students.

Index Card Journal

Journal responses are one way to empower student voice for teachers who prefer quiet, individual ways. Index cards serve as excellent formats for collecting student voice. Because they are small, students perceive them as more "doable."

Browse through this chapter for 4 minutes.
Just see what "pops out at you."
If we were going to spend our entire time during this unit on just
TWO things ~ what would YOU recommend? Why?

1. _____
_____
_____

2. _____
_____
_____

Thanks for taking the time to give an honest answer.

Coaching for this strategy sets the stage for students to maximize their 4 minutes and not just put down the first two things they see. Help them see that you intend to "listen" to what they put down. Although you may wind up with more than two power standards, their voice counts on what the list winds up looking like.

KWL

As an individual or as a pair, ask students to do the first two columns of a K/W/L chart: what you already **K**now (prove it); what looks **W**orth knowing, and what you have **L**earned. (It only takes once to realize that asking what you "want" to know may only get you some answers you'd rather not hear.) Coaching students through this activity would involve helping them recognize that chapter subtitles and words in bold may be "hints" as to degree of value; that they could look at the end of the chapter for additional hints, or read the introduction. Learning to separate "must knows" from "nice to knows" not only preps students for the power standards, but is also a valuable thinking strategy in itself. (A KWL worksheet is provided on the next page.)

KWL **WORKSHEET**

This Unit is About _____   **Your Name** _____

From the materials provided and this chapter, we already KNOW...

Skim through the materials/chapter and describe what you already KNOW.

How could you prove it? We will be able to shorten or eliminate time on items we can prove we already know. Yea!

From the materials provided and this chapter, the following items look WORTH KNOWING...

Skim through the materials/chapter and describe what terms, topics, and concepts appear to be "power standards" WORTH learning, using, and remembering forever.

Look for visual "clues" such as bold type, pictures, or questions.

Here is how we could prove we LEARNED it...

If we are going to spend time only on "what matters most" and if we are to help each other learn in ways that matter, then: What ideas do you have for how we could prove we LEARNED it?

K	**W**	**L**

Unit Organizer

The <u>Strategic Instruction Model</u> (SIM) out of the University of Kansas Center for Research in Learning has created a *Unit Organizer Routine* that provides a blank unit form used with students to introduce and maintain the big ideas in units, and shows how units, critical information and concepts are related from unit to unit. This graphic organizer walks students through 8 steps in preparation for the unit:

1) Students write down the unit title and "guess" what will be most important.

2) and 3) Students write down the title of the previous unit and the chapter to follow. The conversation becomes, "What might we have already learned that seems like it might be useful? What will we need to learn in this unit that seems like it might be needed for the upcoming unit?"

4) Students are asked to think about how these chapters tie together and fit with the big picture.

5) Students are provided a space to create a visual interpretation of the power standards within the unit.

6) Based on the "conversation" so far, students identify thinking and learning strategies that might help them master the material within the unit.

7) Students predict some self-test questions that would "prove" they understand and can use the power standards.

8) Students are involved in developing their own pacing guide for completion of the unit work.

Students of teachers who used the *Unit Organizer Routine* regularly and consistently scored an average of 15 percentage points higher on unit tests. <u>www.kucrl.org/sim</u> An altered form, adapted from the SIM model, is provided on the following page.

Unit ORGANIZER

Unit Organizer For _____ (Course, Teacher)	**Date** _____	
Your Name _____	**Period** _____	

4. The Bigger Picture _____

_____

2. Last Unit/Experience	**1. Current "Unit" Title**	**3. Next Unit/Experience**

8. Unit Schedule

Date	Activity

5. Unit Map

7. Unit Self-Test Questions

6. Thinking Strategies

Adapted from the SIM Model www.kucrl.org/sim

Jigsaw Scouting

Divide students into several teams of three. One team looks at the questions at the end of the chapter. One team looks at the vocabulary list. One team looks at chapter subheadings, words in bold, and picture captions. Other teams divide the pages of the text, and skim through their designated page section. The goal of all teams is to **identify power standards** (What matters most?).

Teams then create a visual of their list, and all the visuals are compared, looking for similarities. A great addition is for you to have created your own list, and let them include yours in the comparison.

Coaching students through this activity becomes especially important during the comparison. The goal is to create one list as a WHOLE team. In the beginning, your role is frequently helping students understand how to separate the "must knows" from the "nice to knows." Since you will know the timeframe for the unit, you can determine what additions of interest to them you can add to the list.

The Actual Test

Now, here's a non-traditional, but effective strategy. Throw out the low-level, multiple-choice, end-of-chapter test, and replace it with a five question, rigorous, open-response exam, where questions require high-level interpretation/application responses, and require depth and detail. HAND THEM THE EXAM. Place three students at three large charts labeled:

Chart 1: WORDS AND TERMS we would need to master

Chart 2: CONCEPTS AND IDEAS we would need to master

Chart 3: QUALITY OPEN RESPONSE will be addressed in Step on page 60.

Have students read Question 1.

Now have them highlight in one color "words/terms" we would need to master to answer this question correctly. Then have them call out what they have highlighted while one student at that chart writes down the term/word in large, clear writing.

Next, ask students to read Question 1 again and highlight in a different color concepts and ideas they would need to master to answer this question correctly. Then have them call out what they have highlighted while a second student at the second chart writes down the concepts/ideas in large, clear writing.

Notice that the students have now read the question three times. The coaching comes into play by making sure that even words like "analyze" (stem words) get put on the list, and that students come to recognize underlying concepts hidden within the question.

The two large charts you have created become, in essence, the power standards within this unit. They can be left posted predominantly in the room throughout this chapter. As the whole class masters words and concepts, they can be visually crossed off so that the class sees how they are progressing toward mastery on key elements that will prepare them to be successful on the final unit exam.

This is a *risky* strategy **only** in that some faculty curmudgeon will insist it is akin to "cheating," because students have been shown the exam. Cheating could only take place IF:

- Students kept the exam and actually remembered to look at it.

- Students took the time to create and remember the open responses that answered these questions correctly, and at a high level.

- Students remembered to review the questions and their answers prior to the actual exam.

Hmmmmmm. Does research support this as a good thing? *(yes!)* Nonetheless, feel free to take up the five questions after Day1.

In involving the students in *scouting the unit*, you have begun to build brain and heart engagement in the battle that is about to take the field. Now, you need to look at scouting the talent that is in the room.

KEY POINT

Scouting the Players (Students)

Having made sure every member of the team has struggled with constructing a picture of what is worth learning and why, next comes the opportunity to discover multiple intelligences, multiple learning styles, multiple interests, and multiple needs OF the students, WITH THE STUDENTS.

The conversation that now begins to take place revolves around gaining student voice in answering the following questions:

- **What should we emphasize?**
- **How should we learn it?**
- **How could we make it more interesting?**
- **What kind of support will we need?**
- **How can we "prove" we learned it?**

What should we emphasize?

An important learning strategy is in helping students determine what topics deserve more time, either because they are challenging or because they are interesting.

How should we learn it?

You don't have to go home and create a lesson plan to address the wide diversity of learners in any one classroom. In a coaching classroom, student voices quickly describe preferences for the one or two choices you provide, and you begin to learn which students are drawn to which strategies.

How could we make it more interesting?

I knew I had fully embraced the coaching framework for my classroom the first time I was able to respond to the comment, "Aw, Miss, this looks boring," with "Really? Okay. Design some way we could make it more interesting and share that with us tomorrow. Will you need a partner?"

What kind of support will we need?

The premise in the coaching framework is that ALL OF US HELP ALL OF US get to mastery. In this scenario, information is power. The more you know about the students in the room, the more you can strategize about how to help the team win. Face it, there are no secrets in a classroom. Students know who's who and what's what. The better they come to know each other's interests and perspectives, the more they will understand, empathize, and help each other.

What you would want and need to know about your students may vary from unit to unit, but some examples might be:

- Who's outgoing and who's shy?
- Who loves math and who doesn't?
- Who has artistic ability?
- Who likes to write?
- Who forgets to turn in homework and who remembers?
- Who likes dancing and music?
- Who likes sports?
- Who likes puzzles?
- Who likes fixing things?
- Who likes technology?

I have frequently observed traditional cooperative learning groups with a project in which team assignments were divvied up as follows:

- You're the outgoing one. You give the presentation.
- You're the artist. You make the graphics.
- You're the teacher's pet. You write the report.

In a coaching classroom, conversations more likely to take place would be:

- You're outgoing and she's shy. You coach her because she's giving the presentation
- You love technology. You teach him how to create a spreadsheet or chart for that information.

When support is student-driven, the person providing the support learns to more depth as well. When support is teacher-DRIVEN, rather than merely teacher-OFFERED, you are taking on the role of *coach*. An important function of the teacher as coach is sharing with the students what you can and will do to provide support. Likewise, let them tell YOU what your role could be in supporting them to get over a higher bar.

Ultimately, the scouting process should be about building connections. The philosophy behind building connections is simple ~ relationships matter. We all work harder for people with whom we feel connected; and we all understand material better when it is connected to something we are interested in.

Connecting to YOU

This is NOT about being a pal to your students. It *is* about showing a genuine interest in each student enough to learn his or her strengths and weaknesses, likes and dislikes. It is about sharing enough mutual information that you feel you know each other better.

Share your own background and love for the subject you teach AND share your own struggle and lack of passion for another subject area. If you are better at math than you are at drawing, say so. If you like reading more than you like math, say so. Let them know that you, too, have areas of strength and weakness, areas of likes and dislikes. Let them know that when you tackle a task for which you feel less motivated, it is much, much harder and that you intend to honor the effort they put out, if your subject is "not their thing."

Connecting to Them

Surprise them! How much can you find out about them before they arrive? Get to know about them personally: have them write a journal entry about how they feel about the class and write them back; call their parents to learn more about them and remember it; know their birthdays and the name they go by; discover their avocations and career dreams, and don't make fun. (See the following page for a sample bulletin board for accomplishing this purpose.)

Get to know them academically. Do you know their reading score? It is available in the office. How well do they understand English (as opposed to pretend to understand)? Do they have a "special need?" Give a pre-test *just* to see what they might know about your subject, or rank how they might feel about certain units. This information is not so that you can *love them into low expectations*, but so that you can strategize about how to get them over the bar.

Let them know that no matter how they feel about your subject, you intend to work with them to make it palatable. Let them know it is YOUR job, and that as a WHOLE GROUP everyone will be able to help everyone else "get it," while also making it more relevant.

Alfie Kohn puts it this way. "The idea is for the teacher to think about what these students need (emotionally speaking) and probably haven't received. That way, we can see 'the vulnerable child behind the bothersome or menacing exterior.'"

Practicing & **POTENTIAL**

After teaching his ninth grade students the meaning of "avocation" and "vocation," one science teacher posted this reflection of their interests and dreams on his bulletin board. He said it helped him to remember to make content connections for the students in his class.

Avocations	**VOCATIONS**
cars	**doctor**
travel	**lawyer**
hunting	**rap star**
football	**basketball**
rodeo	**neonatal nurse**
dancing	**teacher**
music	**engineer**
science fiction	**GPS technician**
photography	**psychologist**
movies	**computer scientist**
herbatology	**carpentar**

Connecting the Class to Each Other

This is also NOT about students running amok. You remain in control of a collaborative group rather than trying to be in control of 35 different individuals all at once. You must have absolutely no tolerance for students *"disrespecting"* other students, **even in jest**. The best way to ensure that the whole class is connected is to never provide an opportunity for any cartels to be established, and to be sure to provide plenty of opportunities for students to learn more about each other.

The overall objective is to establish familiarity and cohesiveness. We have more in common than we do in differences. We may have different strengths and weaknesses, but we ALL have strengths and we ALL have weaknesses. Create a sense of "we're in this together, and though it might be hard, it might be fun." The whole purpose is to help them understand that through a team effort, not only will everyone succeed, but that everyone will exceed at a <u>higher level</u>.

Continue to address the importance of healthy and productive working teams (study buddies, study teams, whole class, tutoring partners, etc.) throughout the class.

Connecting to Other Classes

If you are lucky enough to be at a school that encourages colleagues to become aware of ~ and perhaps even align - power standards in other subject areas, you are a step ahead! It is as simple as letting students know, **with specific examples**, that what you are learning together will be useful in their other classes. It's about letting students bring *you* ideas from their other classes that you might integrate into an upcoming unit. And, on an exciting level ~ BUT ONLY IF IT IS DESIGNED WITH **STANDARDS-FIRST** PRIORITIES ~ it could involve collaborative projects that allow multiple teachers to have groups of students master the unit standards in a more thorough, more complex, *more lasting* way.

Connecting to Interests

Again, we are NOT talking about spending days and weeks off-topic as we build a knowledge base. Just like there are learning styles inventories a student can take in around ten minutes that give you an estimate of their learning preferences, there are versions of the Holland Interest Inventory, or other aptitude or interest surveys, that take around 10-15 minutes and provide you with some information on students' abilities/interests.

Or, you could just ask!

RESEARCH ANCHOR

"...learner-centered principles... recognize that individual learners construct their own personally meaningful, goal-directed understandings of any content or experiences to be learned. Each individual constructs different meaning and understanding based on prior experiences, knowledge, and a host of other personal 'filters.'"

McCombs, 2005

One teacher has four questions on her own survey:

1. Of all the classes you have ever taken, what have been some of your favorite subjects?

2. Of all the classes you have ever taken, what have been some of your worst or least favorite subjects?

3. List five things you do now for fun or would like to do for fun, and only list what you are willing for me to show the principal ~ no middle school or show-off answers!

4. List every job out there in the future that ever sounded interesting to you (remember the principal/middle school thing).

This allows her just enough information to strategize about support and interests.

Connecting to Real Life

The truth is we often don't know enough about how to answer their question, "How am I ever gonna use this?" With a set of yellow pages and a few lists, the class can determine where we might find out or whom we might bring in. Don't forget to include folks majoring in the subject at nearby post-secondary destinations. You won't have to or don't have to do this with every unit, but through the coaching framework you will know when it is important to take half a period to begin to make this happen. I know some teachers who do, however, include a quick guest with every unit now because over the past couple of years their own classes have worked to establish an "Answer Bank" Speakers Bureau for answering this important question at the beginning of every unit.

Connecting to Technology

Today's kids either love technology already, or need to master technology usage. Use it as often as you can, but always in a standards-based application. (Beware: Taking three days to insert animated graphics and sound into a PowerPoint on a unit topic may be much more about the than the animation than the content.) On your initial data sheet, find out who has e-mail. Create an e-group. Allow students who do not have a computer at home *monitored* access to your classroom computer, or to a library computer. Let students help you discover technological applications of course content.

IN SUMMARY Building connections is the "OPENING SALVO," because building relationships is the first, most important ammunition in winning the minds and hearts of a classroom. Regardless of which ways you choose to do it, simply make sure you take time to CONNECT:

- to YOU   let them know you will "coach" them with time, honesty, and a positive attitude

- to the CLASS   they deserve to know what to expect and how it will work

- to CLASSMATES   they should feel comfortable enough within your room to take necessary risks

- to OTHER CLASSES   prove the usefulness and applications of what you teach to other classes they take

- to INTERESTS   use course content in contextual situations that relate to their current interests

- to "REAL" LIFE   continue to illustrate, concretely, course applications to today and tomorrow

- to TECHNOLOGY   use software/hardware, video/audio to allow students to interact with course content

STRATEGIES for Scouting the Kids

**LEARNING MORE
ABOUT THE
STUDENTS**

Whether you "scout"
kids in ways that
involve students as
individuals, teams, or
the whole class is up to
the style of the teacher.
The samples provided
illustrate the variety of
both style and
information you can
gather, prior to
beginning the unit or
chapter.

Pre-Test

I am surprised at how many classrooms head straight into unit lessons without determining the most important information of all. Where are the students now, in comparison to where they should be at the end? If you haven't done a K-W-L or some other indicator of the academic strengths and weaknesses of the students, in direct relation to the power standards in the unit, a power standards pre-test is in order. Consider having the STUDENTS design it after you have completed scouting the unit.

Introductions ~ How are they going to get to know each other?

You can do a simple survey, and set a performance standard from day one, even on this. If you ask them to list their three favorite movies and they list two, return the list to them the next day with a little post-it note arrow pointing to that line, with "I need one more movie."

You can have them review someone else's survey and then use that to further "interview" the person. They can introduce themselves or each other.

There are tons of ideas out there - but don't do the ones that take four days to make a collage in class. The point is simply to learn who comes from big families, or who's an only child; who likes cars; who works after school; etc. Just make sure to do something that helps you build your knowledge base on each individual student in the class, and helps them build their knowledge base and respect for the rest of the class.

One-On-One Interview

Nothing is as thorough or sends a more important message than taking the time to interview students one-on-one to gather knowledge and information that will help you teach them better. Very time consuming but very powerful. Have a list of questions drawn up first. Trade "subbing" during prep periods with another teacher to allow each of you to do this.

Center for Teaching
The Westminster Schools

Parent Talk ~ Friend Talk ~ Self Talk

It is important to find out the support systems kids have, from within and without. Part of the surveys or journal topics used can address whether their parents help encourage and monitor (a lot easier for those kids); whose best friend actually does homework; and identifying habits that make mastering course content easier or harder. The point is NOT to make any judgments, but to let them know that this will help as you strategize about ways to accomplish your unit mission.

Note Cards for Processing

Cut 3x5 index cards in half. Give one to each student (and yourself). Have them write their first and last name on the card. Then, under their name, have them write an interest/hobby they have. Collect the cards and tell the students that you will use them to ask for responses that will have three features: (1) you will ask questions of the class at random, (2) you will ask the student selected to apply the new learning to their area of interest, and (3) you will always ask two students in a row the same question.

Procedure: As you begin a discussion, pick up the deck and shuffle as you ask a question. Say the person's name that appears on the top card and ask them to relate the question you have asked to the interest area they have written on the card. Assist only as needed, as this is "brain processing time." While this student is thinking of how to use/apply the learning of today's lesson, other students now have time to consider their responses, should they be called upon next. In this way, there is far more "work" being done in the minds of learners than if they "spectate" the one who was called on only (typically, when we call on a student for a response, many others will *let them do the work* and only pay peripheral attention. This way, many more are not only paying attention, they are actually doing some of the work required to form memory.

Note: This is effective when used only 2-3 times to start the discussion. After a few times, collect new cards with names and someone they admire, their favorite music, etc. ~ to keep the responses more novel over time.

Go Both Ways Template

Sometimes a reluctant or resistant mind needs to explore "what's wrong" before it can be freed to entertain constructive notions toward improvement. This activity invites the learner to explore reasons for failure as a precursor to determining ways to make things better. It is paradoxical, yet often productive.

Go-Both-Ways ~ **Moving "Back" to Get Ahead**

Select a Situation, Skill, or Circumstance you are Encountering

In this box, enter a description of a long-term assignment that will take 4 weeks to complete, an upcoming gathering with classmates, or a game against a rival opponent.

CREATING Failure	**BUILDING Success**
What 2 things can YOU do to make failure more likely?	What 2 things can YOU do to make success more likely?
1.	1.
2.	2.
What 2 things can a PARENT or TEACHER do to make failure more likely for you?	What 2 things can THEY do to make success more likely for you?
1.	1.
2.	2.
What 2 things can FRIENDS or SCHOOLMATES do to make failure more likely for you?	What 2 things can THEY do to make success more likely for you?
1.	1.
2.	2.

Donegan, Greenleaf, and Wells-Papanek, 2006

Attitude Barometer

One teacher created a **"happiness" scale** to measure how students feel about an assignment or activity. Although light-hearted, the intent of the barometer was to allow him to accurately measure the pressure in the room and coach students to strategize accordingly.

- **Active Crying**   completely discouraged and frustrated
- **Silence**   depressed/disengaged
- **Profanity #@!**   frustrated/angry
- **Bad**   bored/stumped
- **Not Too Bad**   puzzled but hopeful, not completely bored
- **Good**   mildly interested, fairly willing
- **Great**   this might be fun, I think I'll do it
- **Terrific!**   interested and challenged
- **Fantastic!!**   very interested, raring to go
- **Ecstatic!!**   I have always wanted to do this! It sounds hard but really fun!!

Bulletin Boards

Try using either of these two bulletin boards in your class to help "keep you honest." Make sure students are aware of them, and refer to them as you begin each unit.

Everything
We learn together in class will fall into at least one of the following 7 categories:

Check Me, Ask Me, Challenge Me, Help Me ~ Which Ones? How Much? Enough? Too Much?

1. What is truly useful to you **NOW**
2. What is interesting to you **NOW**
3. What is really fun for you **NOW**
4. What is interesting and fun *for me*
5. "Some Day You Will Thank Me" lessons
6. What's directly related to *YOUR* future
7. Necessary "Real World" Nonsense
   district, state, college, jobs, government...

If it is true that we learn...

10% of what we read

20% of what we hear

30% of what we see

50% of what we see and hear

70% of what we discuss

85% of what we experience personally

95% of what we teach someone else

THEN...

How much are we learning by what we do in here TODAY?

Yellow Pages

One teacher keeps a set of ten Yellow Pages in his room. He poses the question to students, **"How IN THE WORLD are we ever going to use what we learn in this unit?"** Students are then given 15 minutes to create a list from the phone book of places they could call to get this question answered. OR, have students do an in-school "Ask around" activity with teachers and older students, to answer that question. OR, have the kids write letters, or make phone calls, or send emails. Invite people in. *Discover **together** the answer to that question!*

Charting the Course

Have students individually rank order the power standards, in terms of "level of difficulty." Now, have students get in common groups based on the similarity of their top two. These groups design support plans and estimate the classroom time and outside-of-classroom time it may take to master these two standards.

The Game of School Students know the difference between a well-prepared athletic team facing a challenging opponent after strategizing ways to gain victory, and the "game playing" that frequently is a daily survival mode of learning environments they find unchallenging or unimportant. One "game" is worth taking the field for. The other is not worth getting up for. The goal of a coaching classroom is to move students out of "playing school" and on to a field where relevant and rigorous challenges await. And perhaps the ultimate measure of success in a coaching classroom is when students no longer see school as an individual battle, but as a team adventure.

In a coaching classroom, transparency and trust are of utmost importance. Since students will be asked to take ownership in their own learning, they need to become versed in "teacher talk." Not only should they know how to define and spot a power standard, they should develop a language that includes learning and thinking strategies (jigsaw, guided inquiry, Socratic Seminar, double entry journaling, mind maps, authentic assessment, etc.). The more options they learn, the more articulate they can become in classroom conversations about learning.

Likewise, some teachers mistake activity for learning. In a coaching classroom, it is important to always keep the targeted mission of each unit in mind, and to make sure each activity directly relates to accomplishing the mission. Involve your students in understanding the "process talk" of such words and phrases as mastery, assessment, targeted mission, collaborative/purposeful activity, etc.

It is even more challenging to coach them to begin to think globally about what "works" and doesn't work (in general as well as specifically for each of them) in turning school as we know it into school as it should be.

One of the most thought-provoking books recently released on changing the instructional paradigm is Robert Fried's *The Game of School: Why We Play It, How It Hurts Kids, and What It Will Take to **Change It***. (Fried, 2005)

Defining Personal Learning ~ Together

Consider having students read Fried's prelude, and discuss what "authentic learning" ~ defined as student engagement in ideas, concepts, skills, and activities that mean something to them, and that lead both to a deeper understanding and to the ability to put ideas to work" would LOOK like, SOUND like, and FEEL like in your classroom.

At the very least, pull relevant quotes from this text to provoke discussion and shake up the norm. Students, like teachers, will revert to the safety of "school as usual," unless reminded and encouraged to create a different reality.

IN SUMMARY **Through *scouting the kids* and involving them in identifying supports, increasing their own responsibility for "making it interesting," and helping them understand the relationship between time and difficulty ~ you have continued to build engagement of the brain and heart.**

Barbara Given implores that unless a classroom climate that is conducive to a sense of emotional safety and personal relevancy for students is established, children will not learn effectively, and may reject our efforts regarding their education altogether.

However, in our sample 15-day unit timeline, the traditional teacher is one day ahead of you in the race for coverage ~ especially since you have two more goals in pre-game preparation before taking the field.

Step TWO ~ *"Begin with the End in Mind"*

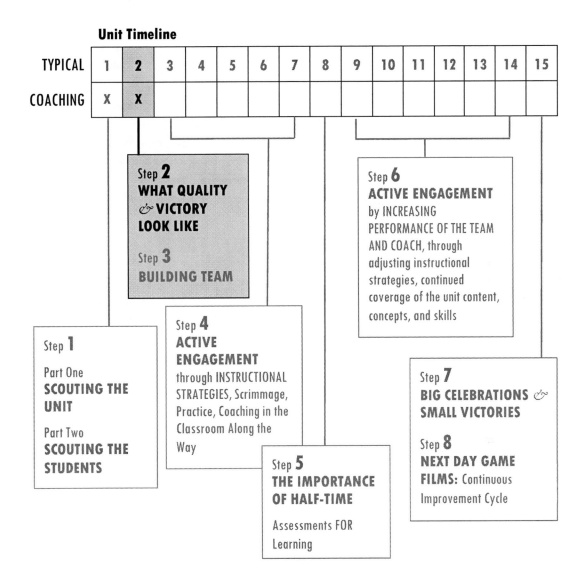

Unit Timeline

TYPICAL	1	2	3	4	5	6	7	8	9	10	11	12	13	14	15
COACHING	X	X													

Step 2
WHAT QUALITY & VICTORY LOOK LIKE

Step 3
BUILDING TEAM

Step 6
ACTIVE ENGAGEMENT by INCREASING PERFORMANCE OF THE TEAM AND COACH, through adjusting instructional strategies, continued coverage of the unit content, concepts, and skills

Step 1
Part One **SCOUTING THE UNIT**
Part Two **SCOUTING THE STUDENTS**

Step 4
ACTIVE ENGAGEMENT through INSTRUCTIONAL STRATEGIES, Scrimmage, Practice, Coaching in the Classroom Along the Way

Step 7
BIG CELEBRATIONS & SMALL VICTORIES

Step 8
NEXT DAY GAME FILMS: Continuous Improvement Cycle

Step 5
THE IMPORTANCE OF HALF-TIME
Assessments FOR Learning

WHO IS DOING THE WORK?

I have a good friend, Ginny, who cares about students deeply, and works hard at being a good teacher. As an English teacher, you will see her after school, dragging the rolling cart behind her, with stacks of essays on their way home to be graded. She has the fastest turn-around time known to mankind. On the very day essays are turned in, her cart is lifted into and out of the trunk of her car, and she proceeds to stay up until way past midnight, reading every word of every essay thoughtfully and objectively, writing voluminous insightful comments and tips about how to be a better writer. Presto! ~ the essays are back on the students' desks the next morning, ripe for review!

It is usually on such a day when there is a knock at my classroom door after school, and all she can manage to say is, "I need a margarita." So off we go for queso and conversation, and I hear a refrain she seems to repeat frequently on days like these. "What's wrong with these kids? I can't believe I stayed up and worked so hard. They barely even glanced at them. A fourth of the essays were left on their desk or in the trash when the bell rang!"

If Einstein's definition of insanity is doing the same thing over-and-over but expecting different results, Ginny's mental state may be more than exhaustion. The overriding quality control question in the coaching classroom is always, "Who's doing the work and the thinking?"

When the pace involves two essays a week in an effort to cover the *Lit Book* and improve writing, it would be hard to turn this thinking/working/grading over to students. Yet, even the National Council of Teachers of English (NCTE) consistently pleads for a general awareness that the slow *writing and rewriting of a single essay until it reaches quality* is a much more effective learning tool than the writing of multiple essays.

Another scenario involves a science teacher friend, Paul, whose frustration was in the fact that so many students had turned in what he so delicately called, "crappy lab reports." "How in the he*! did so many fail?! I gave them an absolutely crystal clear and simple rubric for how to do a quality lab report. Any idiot could have followed those six criteria and passed." Paul's frustration level was so high, I guessed it was not the appropriate time to ask, "Who did the thinking and the work of determining what a good lab report looks like?"

Early explorers benefited from knowledge about where they were headed. "A compass has 360 degrees on it. If you don't know where you are going, then you have 359 chances of not getting there." (anonymous)

Students, too, need to know what direction the unit is headed or chance are they will *not* arrive where you want them to at the end of the unit. Teachers need to articulate IN ADVANCE what achievement targets they want their students to hit. "When they assess FOR learning, teachers use the classroom assessment process and the continuous flow of information about student achievement that it provides in order to advance, not merely check on, student learning... They do this by understanding and articulating *in advance of teaching* the achievement targets that their students are to hit and by informing their students about those learning goals, *in terms that students understand*, **from the very beginning** of the teaching and learning process." (Stiggins, 2002)

When Stephen Covey set out his *7 Habits of Highly Effective People*, he offered this advice: "Begin with the End in Mind." In other words, work backwards from where you want to end up, and make choices that will lead you there. If we are expecting students to master and maintain essential knowledge and skills from our unit, we will need to provide an assessment at the end of the unit. But, in far too many classrooms that end of unit "test" is either a secret, or a surprise. Students may know it is coming but they have no clue what it looks like. Even less likely, is that they have had any say in what it looks like. Students must be let in on the assessment process, and even more importantly, on the secrets of assessing themselves throughout the *season* ~ all along the way.

KEY POINT

"Begin with the End in Mind"

In his article, "*Assessments without Victims*," Rick Stiggins points out that when students are involved in the assessment process they can come to see themselves as competent learners. "We need to involve students by making the targets clear to them and having them help design assessments that reflect those targets. Then we involve them again in the process of keeping track over time of their learning so they can watch themselves improving. That's where motivation comes from." (Stiggins, 2003)

The important point is in helping students understand and "own" clearly what mastery looks like PRIOR to beginning the unit/assignment.

RESEARCH ANCHOR

Setting Goals has been shown to have a potential, overall impact of a +23% increase in academic achievement compared to when goal setting is not used.

Marzano et. al., 2001

There are several tough questions to ask ourselves about the culminating assessment OF learning for our coaching classroom unit:

- The first and most important question sequence is: Have kids seen it? Do they know what it looks like? Do they know when it is? Do they know how to prepare for it? Do they know what good answers would look like?

- The second most important question sequence is: Do students have a personal stake in it? Have they had a voice in what gets asked, and how it gets graded?

- Is it a power standards assessment? In other words, do we have confidence that the questions being asked are questions worth knowing the answers to... forever? I've seen some teachers take an existing test and simply circle the questions that are most worth knowing, and cross through questions that may not represent their unit power standards. Now, imagine what that experience could become if you did it *with* the kids?

Will the ability to do well on this assessment challenge students at more than a recall level? Again, if we are talking about involving students, the possibility arises that students could rewrite the existing essential test questions to a higher level on Bloom's Taxonomy. They would now be involved in eliminating some test questions altogether, in exchange for creating a smaller set of questions where the level of thinking and responding was "a more worthy opponent."

RESEARCH ANCHOR

"We're used to jumping to lesson and activity ideas - before clarifying our performance goals for students. [However] By thinking through the assessments upfront, we ensure greater alignment of our goals and means, and that teaching is focused on desired results."

Wiggins and McTighe, 2002

- Are there aspects of the assessment for which a rubric is going to be used? If so, then what role does the student have in designing the scoring guide? We all understand that students perform at higher levels if they have ownership of their work, but we seldom apply this to end of unit assessment. Our job as a coach is to create an atmosphere of achievement and accomplishment, where the students can take pride in having fashioned their own formula for assessment.

Let's be absolutely clear. Many teachers will falsely assume this practice is going to lower expectations, as students either get to "see" the questions ahead of time, or ~ even worse ~ write the test questions. The opposite is true.

What we are trying to accomplish, first of all, is to develop the ability to **work backwards from where you want to end up, and to make choices that will lead you there.** Depending on the unit and the destination, you may or may not choose to involve students in creating the assessment, but you *will* let them see it, talk about it, and talk about how to do well on it ~ *before leaving the driveway.* It is that awareness of the destination that will help you, together, know where to stop and for how long. Secondly, you are helping them build an awareness of what QUALITY looks like.

KEY POINT

The Importance of Exemplars

As we noted earlier, students will not eagerly jump at the opportunity to set high standards for themselves. Not only are they used to the path of least resistance, they are used to teachers handing them the "how to make an 'A'" form. When asked to describe quality for themselves, they are frequently at a loss.

But rather than falling into the trap of describing it for them, let's coach them to grapple with this important issue. One way to support them in this effort is to provide them with an exemplar of student work from a different class/year (not this class!). Give them visible, tangible examples of what good work looks like, and then help them parse out what it is that makes it "good." The time spent on this prior to the unit will not only move you toward capturing their brains and hearts, it will also result in a greater likelihood of you actually winding up with quality in the end.

What if my friend Paul had given students an example of a quality lab report, and asked pairs of students to identify the three most important qualities in the lab report that he would be looking for, and that students thought were worth doing? The coaching comes in the "negotiable contracting," as students piece together the criteria that ultimately get you more compliance and higher results. Would it be easier and faster to do it yourself? Undoubtedly. However, student involvement up front will result in a classroom climate where more students have clarity and commitment surrounding "quality."

STRATEGIES for "Begin with the End in Mind"

CLARIFYING KEY LEARNING TARGETS

The samples provided focus on ways teachers can help students understand more exactly what the ultimate expectation for success looks like so that they have more motivation and more clarity as they begin to tackle the unit or chapter.

The Actual Test

Earlier, we described a classroom where, in scouting the unit, students had seen the "actual test" ahead of time. The teacher had replaced a low-level, multiple choice test with a rigorous, open-response exam, where questions required high-level interpretation and answers required depth and detail. The first chart asked, "What terms would we need to know to do well on the test?" The second chart asked, "What concepts and ideas would we need to master to do well on the test?" **The third chart asks, "What would a high quality, open-response answer 'look like'?"**

Students were provided with an exemplar, and then began to describe what they were seeing. They began by being as specific as the number of sentences, the length of the sentences, and the quality of the words and grammar within the sentences. They moved on to the use of terms, and the way terms were defined in context. Then they talked about how concepts and ideas were introduced and supported. They talked specifically about detail, and the organization of that detail as it supported ideas. They wound up their discussion talking about how each answer "began" and "ended." The descriptors were then posted along with the other two charts, prominently displayed on the wall, for reference during the unit.

KWL Revisited

There was also a third column on the K-W-L chart we used with students, which had a different adaptation than the typical post-unit interpretation, "What did you learn?" On this chart, the column reads, "How could we **prove** we learned it? If we are going to spend time only on 'what matters most,' and help each other learn what matters most in ways that matter ~ what ideas do you have for how we could prove we LEARNED it?"

This invites students to suggest alternate assessments to the typical end-of-unit exam. You will begin to discover that students will identify ~ even before they know the "teacher talk" ~ artifacts, performance assessments, oral presentations, demonstrations, exhibitions, portfolios, as well as a variety of traditional testing measures. Completing this column prior to beginning the unit helps students see the connection between the standards they have identified as "worth knowing," and the end result.

Real-World Standards

In pairs or teams of three, have students e-mail or call outside sources, asking for a list of qualities and examples of "quality" on a similar assessment. You could also have your students interview college students or teachers in the building, to add to this list. Teams would share their answers, and then create their own description or rubric identifying quality on the final assessment.

Index Card Question

After collecting these questions, the class could determine how many and which questions would be used, devising their own combination of recall or understanding questions, and analysis, synthesis, or evaluation questions. As the teacher, you could have a list of what you felt were the "important" questions, and students could see how many of those they actually identified, as well. Which ones were missing and why?

Based on what you know is important in this chapter,
if you were going to ask ONE QUESTION that was "worth knowing and remembering forever," what would it be?
Ask it once as a low-level Bloom's question, and then rewrite it as a higher-level, open response question.

1. _____

_____

_____

2. _____

_____

_____

Thanks for taking the time to design our end-of-unit assessment

---

Then, ask the students – in small groups or as a whole class – to devise a real-world, unpredictable, application scenario. Let students determine what percentage this scenario should count in the overall unit test.

Ideally, you will both gradually begin to count the higher-level, open-ended questions to a greater degree, as you develop mutual confidence in their ability to display mastery of the power standards in this way.

Student-Designed Rubrics

We sometimes mistakenly assume that students will recognize quality when shown a rubric. In fact, many students need to be involved in concrete discussions of what quality looks like, and fashion scoring guides in a language that is clear and understandable to them. The following description comes from *The Art of Negotiable Contracting for Assessment,* on a website called Interactive Classroom www.interactiveclassroom.com. (Stix, 2000) "We already know that students perform at higher levels if they have ownership of their work. But the finishing touch to this grand design is to create an atmosphere of achievement and accomplishment where the students can take pride in having fashioned their own formula for assessment... The ideas should come from the students' side of the classroom, making the assessment truly authentic to the task."

More importantly, student-designed rubrics build skills for students to begin mastering the ability to self-assess. Most students will arrive in your classroom having been conditioned to always turn to you to ask "How am I doing?" In a coaching classroom, students begin to ask *themselves* that question, and to use tools to help them make concrete self-assessments. This builds confidence in their ability to meet expectations.

Regardless of whether you follow exactly any of the procedures above, you want to accomplish two goals with students:

1. You have eliminated anxiety and increased clarity, by ensuring they know ahead of time how they will be assessed individually at the end.

2. You have helped students understand and "own" clearly what mastery and quality looks like, PRIOR to beginning the unit/assignment.

Now, it is time to build their confidence even further by letting them know they are not in this alone. Not only you, but the whole class is there as a support, to see that they are successful on this unit. Although we will assess them individually, they will LEARN TOGETHER.

Step THREE ~ *Building Team*

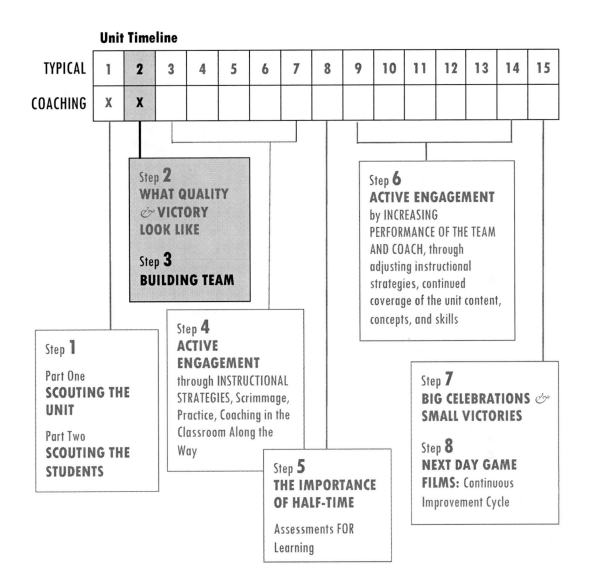

Unit Timeline

	1	2	3	4	5	6	7	8	9	10	11	12	13	14	15
TYPICAL	1	2	3	4	5	6	7	8	9	10	11	12	13	14	15
COACHING	X	X													

Step **2**
WHAT QUALITY
& **VICTORY**
LOOK LIKE

Step **3**
BUILDING TEAM

Step **6**
ACTIVE ENGAGEMENT
by INCREASING
PERFORMANCE OF THE TEAM
AND COACH, through
adjusting instructional
strategies, continued
coverage of the unit content,
concepts, and skills

Step **1**
Part One
SCOUTING THE UNIT
Part Two
SCOUTING THE STUDENTS

Step **4**
ACTIVE ENGAGEMENT
through INSTRUCTIONAL
STRATEGIES, Scrimmage,
Practice, Coaching in the
Classroom Along the
Way

Step **5**
THE IMPORTANCE OF HALF-TIME
Assessments FOR
Learning

Step **7**
BIG CELEBRATIONS *&*
SMALL VICTORIES

Step **8**
NEXT DAY GAME FILMS: Continuous
Improvement Cycle

OVERVIEW

Vince Lombardi stated simply, "People who work together will win, whether it be against complex football defenses, or the problems of modern society." But it is not just the effectiveness of teams that enhances the classroom; it is the attitude shift it creates for the Jasons who reside in it. Knowing that there is a tier of support and a team goal creates a very different outlook in how the unit is approached by previously reluctant learners.

Students whose initial reaction to a challenging assignment is "fight or flight," disengage even further when asked to be solely responsible for their current state, and future work ethic. Their experience with failure and frustration lets them know it is easier just to shut down, or act out.

Fostering a sense of belonging increases academic performance. You can heighten feelings of belonging by building a classroom team. When you build feelings of belonging and safety in your classroom, you increase your ability to engage students' minds. This atmosphere supports the efficient and effective delivery of curriculum.

Let students know that you will learn together, but assess individually. Each student is held individually accountable for the ultimate mastery of unit content, but along the way they are relying on each other to achieve this mastery.

KEY POINT

Team Psychology

If we accept Maslow's hierarchy of needs, then we understand *belonging* to be the most basic need. Unless the need for belonging is met, students get stuck and cannot devote full energy to the intellectual pursuit ahead. Taking the time for team building, prior to the beginning of the unit, has a positive impact on academics because it builds relationships. Sagor points out the connection we want to build for students is, "The more I love the class, the more I love everything associated with it, including the teacher and the content."

The need for power is also addressed in a team setting. Glasser, like Sagor, says that what we need are academic settings in which students, if they work, can gain an immediate sense of power. Unfortunately, the most successful are concentrated in traditionally viewed non-academic areas where it is almost exclusively available through team or group activities such as athletics, music, or drama programs. A traditional classroom design centers on individual effort and individual competition, "a structure that, by its very nature, limits the chances of almost all students to gain not only the power, but also the fun and belonging they all desire." (Glasser, 1986) This does not have to remain the case. A coaching framework treats the class as a team, where all members contribute, and all share in the workload and the victory.

Quality is rarely a do-it-yourself process. We all are more likely to face challenges with "backup." I am much more likely to go to the gym if someone goes with me. With friends, I am more likely to persevere. Like most of us, students will not pursue school subjects in depth; completely on their own, and right now - in almost all classes they are alone. Teamwork gives them the courage to tackle more rigorous assignments that increase in depth and involvement as the course progresses.

RESEARCH ANCHOR

"...without acceptance and emotional support energy needed for developing new skills may be spent seeking positive affirmations and guarding against abuse, ridicule, sarcasm, embarrassment, isolation, loneliness, and rejection."

Given, 2002

RESEARCH ANCHOR

Working together increases trust: "Research has also shown that learning is enhanced in contexts were learners have supportive relationships, have a sense of ownership and control over the learning process, and can learn with and from each other in safe and trusting environments."

McCombs and Whisler, 1997

We are social creatures; we need the support and interest of others. It is no fun to read a new book or go to a play or movie and then just think about what we saw or read on our own. It is far more likely for us to engage and persevere if we have social and emotional support.

Spencer Kagan, a cooperative learning specialist, notes that another reason why time spent teambuilding prior to the academic activity is successful is based on the nature of attention, and the balance between "taking in" and "putting out." (Kagan, 1999) Team building allows the give and take that keeps motion and emotion active. He asks the question, "Would you rather spend 100 percent of time on academics as students sit half attentive, or 80% of the time on academics, with the students interested, bright-eyed, and 100% attentive?"

The more team building you do, the better students perform individually. The more you create a sense of team, the more students feel a personal connection to "my" classroom. In a coaching framework, individual students have a vested interest in reaching team success.

KEY POINT

GOOD TEAMS...
Don't Just Happen.

They thrive when elements of teamwork are nurtured.

ATTRIBUTES OF A GOOD TEAM

A coaching classroom incorporates the same qualities that create a good athletic team. As you read this description from a winning volleyball coach, think of ways this could be replicated in an academic classroom. And it CAN be replicated. As this coach would tell you himself, it is not volleyball they love as much as they love the volleyball TEAM:

Share a Common Goal

The team (players and staff) must know that they are all in search of a common goal. They must trust and firmly believe that all members of the team will do whatever it takes to reach that goal.

Have a Passion for Excellence

We must have a passion for excellence. This passion needs to extend to every contact with the ball. This passion is at the heart of a strong work ethic in all areas. It should drive us to improve daily.

Have Good Communication

A good team has good communication. There is constant talk about what has just happened, what is likely to happen, and what or how each individual will respond in certain situations. On a good volleyball team, the setter and the hitter are sure to compliment the passer if a good pass was made. The hitter compliments the setter when a good set is made. Neither the setter nor hitter

RESEARCH ANCHOR

"Teachers who nourish the emotional system serve as mentors for students by demonstrating sincere enthusiasm for their subject; by helping students discover a passion for learning; by guiding them toward reasonable personal goals and by supporting them in their efforts to become whatever they are capable of becoming."

Given, 2002

can assume that the other knows what was wrong ~ it must be communicated in a civil fashion. Screaming "higher" at the setter when the ball is set too low is a command ~ not communication. Communication off the court is equally important. Whatever talk there is outside the gym needs to be constructive. If complaining takes place, it is the responsibility of whoever might be listening to not allow it to continue. Talking about a problem with someone with the goal of finding a solution is constructive.

Play With Emotion

A good team plays with emotion. There is a celebration after winning a point or side-out, regardless of how it was won. Teammates draw strength from one another when the going gets tough, and share the joy of hard won victories.

Feed Off Each Other

A good team learns to "feed off each other." A team player will still give to the team, even if she isn't necessarily having a great day performing. If I have not executed a skill perfectly, but my teammates have somehow made a good play out of it, I need to rejoice in our good play, instead of sulking about my error. I can often "make up" for my skill error by the way I choose to act about it. I can always control my attitude. One of the great things about being on a team is the fact that I have teammates that can pick up the slack if I have a bad day. If I learn to feed off my teammates, I can often work through the trouble spots and turn my performance into a positive one.

Enjoy What They Are Doing

On a good team, people take part because they love what they're doing. They take part because they are having fun, benefiting while they are working hard.

Give Extra

Players on a good team put in extra work. They want areas of weakness in their game to become areas of strength. They look forward to the satisfaction from extra time that they might have to work on these areas, and spend the time because teammates are there with them.

All the attributes of a good athletic team work to create good classroom teams as well.

STRATEGIES for Building a Team

WORKING
PRODUCTIVELY
TOGETHER

The samples provided help teachers accomplish a key understanding in coaching classrooms: "We learn together. All of us help all of us succeed."

Share a Common Goal

Michael Korda stated, "Success has always been easy to measure. It is the distance between the team's origins and the team's final achievement." Once trust and team are built, transparency is acceptable and encouraged. After students have identified the power standards that are part of the unit and examined (or developed) the assessment at the end of the unit, they can set individual and group goals for the level of mastery they intend to achieve by the end of the unit.

The individual goal is for each student to improve from the pre-test. The classroom goal is to set a class average you intend to accomplish by the end. 90% of the class will reach 80% or above ~100% of the class will reach 75% or above, etc.

RESEARCH ANCHOR

"Classroom and school norms take on extremely important roles regarding the development of socially acceptable behavior and in learning how to resolve conflicts. School needs to be a place where children get to know one another at a deep level."

Given, 2002

Game Plan

The most important part of building team is to help individual students see that each member, with support, has something valuable to contribute. Talking with students in terms of which students will take the lead on which parts and then help the others learn it, is an important part of the game plan. Helping the students design an approach to the lessons at hand, and divvying up the workload with the common goal that all students will pass this unit is key to the attitude shift you are looking for.

Remember to RECOGNIZE DIFFERENCES and ACKNOWLEDGE EFFORT. Not liking a subject, or not having the same background or interest in a subject as another student, is not about who's smart and who's dumb. Support, applaud, and cheer for those for whom ~ for whatever reason ~ this is harder to do.

Inspiration through Charting Progress

Charting healthy competition between "Period 2" and "Period 3" in IMPROVEMENT is warranted. You can even post team goals and not worry about confidentiality. After the pre-test, the individual score is at a baseline of zero (regardless of if they got a 93 or a 53), and the graph then begins to chart progress. It is important that students, as individuals and part of a team, see a visual representation of the progress ~ whether rate-of-growth or value-added ~ they are making throughout the work on the unit.

Goal Line

Some teachers share the sports theme we've been using throughout initial direct instruction on goal setting, and refer to the space for writing weekly (or unit) goals as the "Goal Line," a specific place that students should aim for in order to feel a sense of accomplishment by the end of the week (or unit).

The teacher should help students create a specific goal at the start of each unit (or designated timeframe) that is measurable. Discuss with students how classroom activities can assist in the successful accomplishment of the goal. Specific activities may need to be adapted or designed at that time, to fit the student needs and goals selected. Once or twice in the beginning, the teacher may want to have everyone select the same goal, and then discuss whole-class strategies for working on the goal.

Your Mission, Should You Decide to Accept It

This strategy can be used as another teamwork exercise to encourage students to buy into course content.

Step One   Discuss the definition and purpose of "mission statements." Students can read and analyze the district and campus mission statements, then read the teacher's mission statement for the class, analyze it, and work in teams to rewrite the mission statement.

Step Two   *Students can create a mission statement for the class or for the unit.*

Step Three   Students can develop a personal mission statement for the class or the unit, and post them by their picture, or on a class bulletin board.

Learning Teams

Some teachers move students within the classroom into small learning teams of two to five students, using the pre-test to ensure that teams cover the range of pre-mastery. The structure within these teams may sometimes call for each team doing the same work and comparing it to other teams; or at other times, call for dividing the work, with teams teaching it to each other. In small groups, you can average the pre-test scores of the members of the group, and again set the baseline at zero and chart learning team progress. The opportunity arises for teams who reach mastery to, in turn, re-teach teams who are not there yet, as part of reaching the whole class goal.

Choose Your Partner

"The problem with group work is...?!?!". The simple fact is that students are easier to "control" when they are working individually at their desk. The reality is that they NEED to learn to work **productively** in teams. In a coaching classroom, the class discusses why and how group work can be effective and ineffective prior to working in groups, then commits to some norms, and learns some structure.

Discuss with the class, *what are the advantages and disadvantages of grouping by:*

- 2 members, 3 members, 4 members or 5 members
- Self-selected? Assigned? or Random?
- "Cliques" and Friends
- Homogeneous ~ boys, ethnicity, clowns, shy, extroverts, overachievers
- Levels on the Pre-test
- Diversity of Interests versus Like Interests
- Distraction/Attention/Concentration issues

Students also need to be prepared ahead of time, to answer important questions related to working in a smaller team:

- How will you know, and what will you do when someone dominates?
- What would a "productive" group look like?
- **How could we "prove" everyone is working?**

Having students recognize ahead of time that learning teams may need to vary depending on the task, and having students plan ahead of time for the most common issues surrounding group work, eliminates most problems.

If many of the classroom activities that students will engage in throughout the year in your class involve teamwork, you will want to take even more time to help students discover what is needed to work in teams. The first exercise could be working in teams *to learn about* how to work in teams! Think-pair-share strategies can be used to have students look at a list of behaviors, and determine whether they are team-building qualities. Use an anticipation strategy to help students figure out why team roles are important, and have them write job descriptions for team roles such as Checker/Gatekeeper, Recorder, Taskmaster, Quartermaster, Coach, and Reporter. You can have students read articles about team building, and apply an appropriate reading strategy exercise. You can even have students watch movie segments where teamwork plays an important role, such as in *Remember The Titans*, and have students analyze and discuss teamwork qualities and roles.

TEAM ROLES Here are some suggested team roles, though you may want to *simplify or combine* some roles for smaller groups.

Checker ~ Gatekeeper

Someone in the group needs to be responsible for checking for understanding of the task, and the contributions. That person can also be the gatekeeper in terms of making sure all members participate.

Recorder ~ Graphics

Someone in the group needs to be responsible for keeping a written record of the ideas and decisions. Sometimes, a graphic artist position is established if those ideas need to be presented in a more creative, visual form.

Taskmaster ~ Quartermaster ~ Timekeeper

These roles have to do with making sure the team stays focused, works within deadlines, and has all appropriate supplies.

Coach

This position involves providing praise and encouragement, and determining when the team needs extra motivation or assistance.

Reporter ~ Orator

Typically, the most outgoing student will want to be the reporter, or will be delegated such by his or her peers. Make sure students rotate through reporter positions. This provides an opportunity for all students to receive additional oral presentation experiences, and is also an opportunity for the more outgoing student to coach another student in presentation skills. If you are new to group work, start with THREE members only: reporter, recorder, taskmaster, or some other combination. In a coaching classroom, the "natural born" reporter would not report each time, but would ~ instead ~ coach the shy member on how to report.

It is important that a clear set of protocols and roles for any team activity be determined. That way, any time students are asked to participate in a group activity, they will be practicing the same set of skills.

Ropes

Some teachers involve students in some parallel teambuilding activities, and then ask them to extrapolate what it would look like in tackling the unit. One of the most commonly used activities for teaching students the value of team to meet challenges is through "ropes courses." One easy version you can do in class is a *Human Knot*:

1. Make sure students know to arrive at class in loose clothes and pants.

2. Divide the class into two groups (a group of 10-16 individuals) facing one another in a tight circle.

3. Each person holds out his/her right hand and grasps the right hand of someone else, as if they were shaking hands.

4. Next each person extends his/her left hand and grasps the hand of someone else, so that each person is holding two different hands.

5. This hand-in-hand configuration should come out equal.

6. The group is to try to unwind themselves from their tangled situation, so that after much try-this, try-that squirming and contorting, a hand-in-hand circle is formed.

7. The physical hand-to-hand contact that you have with your partner cannot be broken in order to facilitate an unwinding movement. Sweaty palms may pivot on one another, but skin contact may not be lost. After some hesitation, members of the group will start to duck under or step over the linked arms of others. Eventually, the group should end up with a big circle of students alternating front to back, or sometimes with two circles. As a result of the initial grasping movements, and depending upon the number of participants, two or even three distinct circles may be formed. These circles are sometimes intertwined like Olympic rings.

8. If the group has been struggling with a "knot" for longer than your class has time, offer an honorable out, called *Knot First Aid*. Indicate that actual hands-and-arms knots do sometimes materialize in this jumble of anatomical parts, and that it may become necessary to effect a cure by deciding, amongst the group, which grip needs knot first aid; i.e., which pair of hands should be separated and re-gripped.

The physical movement and fun involved in this activity breaks down barriers, and creates a sense of camaraderie amongst students who may not previously have interacted. **Then, it becomes very important to discuss how teamwork and problem solving will be applied to the course content.**

Goal Grids ~ for Students, for Teachers, for Class, for Group

It is important to know the difference between a performance goal and an outcome goal, and go for the performance goals! Do not even bother working with goals unless you intend to revisit them on a regular basis, and use them to measure growth. **If you do integrate them thoroughly into the class design, and teach students how to become goal driven, it will have remarkable power in helping students achieve.**

Some direct instruction will be needed on why and how to set goals. There are many resources available that provide information on goal setting, and all agree that achievable goals need to be concrete, performance-based, and have a deadline. One acronym that students find easy to remember and apply is setting goals that are SMART:

Specific	Write your goal in concrete, descriptive terms.
Measurable	How will you be able to prove you accomplished your goal?
Action-Oriented	Don't state an outcome, but state what you will DO.
Realistic	Goals should be a stretch, but reachable.
Timetable	Set a specific date to measure your goal, and incremental dates for actions.

Have students practice writing class goals, and then discuss in class whether the goal fits all the necessary criteria. Rewrite them until they do. When students complete their first weekly "Goal Line," have them check to make sure it is SMART. The teacher should always model behaviors, and set weekly goals that are shared with the class.

Even SMARTer ~ As your class progresses, have students continue to raise the bar for themselves in terms of the level of the goal. Continue to monitor for the five components, check on progress, analyze and revise strategies, and celebrate successes.

Although research says that simply having a concrete goal and writing it down is a big step toward successfully achieving that goal, having a plan and mustering support will increase the likelihood of success. A simple goal grid helps students create a plan that can be recorded in their subject planner, or notebook. A goal grid should contain a place for the date and a goal line for writing a SMART goal.

The grid should contain four components: (see template that follows)

- What are students going to do differently from what they have done in the past, which will help them accomplish this goal? What will increase?

- Sometimes small (or big) sacrifices have to be made to provide time and energy to do the things necessary to achieve their goals. What decisions are students going to make, that illustrate they are able to stop doing something that interferes with the accomplishment of their goals?

- No one should think they have to accomplish a goal without assistance. Where can they go for concrete help? To whom can they turn for moral support? In what ways can people help them accomplish their goals?

The most important skill behind goal-setting is the concept of deferred gratification; making the important discovery that it is fun and profitable to finally reach your goals, even if the hard work along the way didn't necessarily seem that way. Make sure students list, and visualize, external and internal rewards that could result from accomplishing their goal.

An additional part of the grid that student's find enjoyable is to create a motto that ties into the goal's subject matter. This also provides good research and thinking practice.

The first time students are shown the goal grid, the teacher can use his or her own weekly goal as a sample handout on what a grid could contain. Each time, the teacher should set and model goals right along with the students. Use students in your own class in the support square. Have students share and compare grids when they complete them.

Using a goal grid helps students practice this skill. The timeline can be adjusted as your class progresses, and students learn to achieve goals successfully.

At some point, students should have successfully completed several Goal Grids and begun to build a "cycle of success," where they come to appreciate deferred gratification, and look forward to the ultimate reward of a job well done. Once students have experienced several instances of the good feelings and concrete compensation from achieving goals, patience, and perseverance are more easily exhibited. Now, it is time to encourage students to stretch themselves, in terms of setting higher and more difficult goals.

Goal Grids ~ **FOR STUDENTS, TEACHERS, CLASSES, AND GROUPS**

Goal _____

Subject Matter   Unit Topic

Write your goal.

Be prepared to be able to prove it.

Specific	I will	_____
Measurable	By	_____
Action-Oriented	By	_____
Realistic		_____
Timetable	Within	_____

This is what I will add:	This is what I will give up:
This is my support system:	**This is my reward:**

... and this is the motto that will inspire me when I want to give up:

Donegan, Greenleaf, and Wells-Papanek, 2006

In *Telling Stories of Change*, McCombs quotes a student, "This is the first class I've ever had where they asked us questions, like, you know: 'Guys, how do you feel about doing this? How does this work in what you're doing? Does this help you out? Will this help you remember for the essay test?' It's not the same as being told 'just sit down and do the work.' "

Our classroom goal is to have ALL students willing to get on the field and in the game. Because of that critical goal, pre-game is the most important ~ and often longest ~ part of the coaching framework. Brain-based research confirms that this time up front will pay off in the learning outcomes.

Research & RESULTS

Goal Setting The process of establishing a direction for learning that identifies both short and long-term objectives.

Goal setting considerations:

1. Narrow the focus of study (however, assure the instruction and assessments are aligned with the overall goals).

2. Maintain a general scope that accommodates the constructivist nature of learning differences (behavioral objectives have less impact, as they are too specific).

3. Student performance increases when they have the opportunity to personalize the "teacher's" overall goals for a unit of study.

Teamwork

Given, 2002

Working WITH others is not the same as working AMONG others, at least not when it comes to engaging the brain fully. …learners [have a need] to interact, to explore ideas and to communicate with others about their ideas. When students are considered a community of learners, they learn to build on the strength of working together to problem-solve, support each other in a constructive environment.

Pre-game preparation does more than just provide a motivational environment for engaging brains and hearts. It is in the pre-game preparation where you create a game plan and coaching-plan that builds the necessary scaffolding for students to climb, as they rise to meet the higher standards of a coaching classroom.

Step THREE Pre-Game ~ Building Team *Checklist for Success*

Questions I should **ask myself** *before each* "unit":

Questions I must **ask the kids** along the way *(knowing I may need to coach them to correct answers):*

☐ **Overriding "Quality Check" Question: Who's doing the work here: me? or the kids?**

☐ What are the <u>POWER standards</u> that EVERY kid MUST know?

☐ Have I "<u>given up</u>" some material in order to teach the Power Standards to ALL?

☐ Have I "<u>ratcheted up</u>" the lesson, assignment, and assessment on the Power Standard?

☐ Have I built in a <u>BRIEF/Pre-Game activity</u> prior to the "work" of the unit?

☐ Have they seen and discussed the <u>ending assessment</u> prior to the "work" of the unit?

☐ Has the class set a "performance goal" as a team and discussed ways to *learn together*?

☐ Is there a plan for charting progress along the way? Is it a "visual" for the individual and class?

☐ Have I built in "<u>try it/talk about it/kick it up a level</u>" (revision to quality) in at least one assignment?

☐ How do they know <u>their opinion matters</u>?

☐ What looks most important and why?

☐ What looks hardest and why?

☐ How does it relate to "real" life?

☐ What should we emphasize?

☐ How should we learn it?

☐ How can we help each other learn it?

☐ What kind of support will we need?

☐ How can we make it more interesting?

☐ How can we "prove" we learned it?

☐ What would quality look like?

In our coaching framework, ON-THE-FIELD, and IN-THE-GAME contains:

Step FOUR ~ *The First Half*

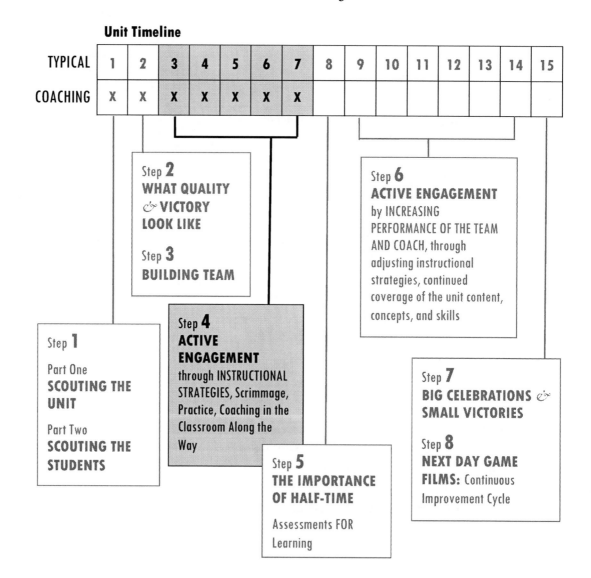

OVERVIEW   In our example of the 15-day unit, our traditional teacher is now *two* days ahead of us as we begin to take the field. Are we behind? Perhaps at the moment; but what we have created is a team of students who understand the destination, their own important role in the journey, and who are willing to work harder, better, faster on the challenges at hand. More brains and more hearts are in the game.

KEY POINT

The First Half

In reality, many coaching classrooms begin simply by inserting pre-game preparation into the unit and lesson plans that already exist. The first "half" of their lessons looks identical to the way they did them previously, but the preparation at the beginning has done more to gather active engagement.

Many of our lessons already exhibit commonalities to coaching classrooms ~ opportunities to learn and practice a skill, opportunities to test the skill out in small venues, and opportunities to receive feedback and advice on how to improve. We may call it lecture, homework, and quizzes, but ~ in fact ~ we are providing coaching, practice, coaching, scrimmages, and coaching. Notably, a few traditional classrooms ~ even though they are on the brink of this framework ~ provide the lecture, homework, and quizzes, but NOT the coaching.

RESEARCH ANCHOR

"The most powerful single modification that enhances achievement is feedback. The simplest prescription for improving education must be 'dollops of feedback'."

Hattie, 1992, in Marzano et. al., 2001

In a power standards unit, where quality is valued over quantity, we require fewer ~ but more engaged, complex, and thoughtful ~ performances from students. The primary coaching role is designed to help students recognize and achieve quality on these performances. This involves ongoing feedback from the teacher, from peers, and from self-evaluation, with multiple opportunities to improve.

Homework assignments become practice opportunities to review and refine skills. Quizzes become scrimmages to provide early and frequent feedback that is diagnostic, rather than evaluative. Informal practice or game sessions are for the purpose of assessing skills and making adjustments. The teacher becomes coach, giving continuous and consistent "advice" and encouragement on how to improve play ~ leading to achievement and success. Former NFL quarterback Roger Staubach remarked on the hard work of practice as a means to success saying, "Spectacular achievements are always preceded by unspectacular practices."

RESEARCH ANCHOR

"Teachers with large gains [in student achievement] were committed to feedback that was consistently accurate, with student performance compared to unambiguous expectations."

Reeves, 2003

Feedback means to provide timely information relative to how well the learner is doing *on identified learning goals & objectives*. Timely feedback is required if adjustments to learning are to take place.

It is this meta-cognitive stage that is most frequently missing in the traditional classroom, where every grade counts, and the first version is all too often the final version. Many students will be making an effort to do quality work for the first time in their lives. They are not likely to reach it the first time. Moving on before they get there is a mistake. Using exemplars, models, and rubrics, students should be actively involved in evaluating others' work, and revising their own work as part of daily practice.

The coach's job is to "stay on them and stay with them" until they experience the joy of doing quality work. **It is much better to work through revisions of a single quality product, than to turn in numerous products of lesser quality.** The learning is in the re-doing, and revisions are seen as much more important than simply grading, and moving on to the next piece of work.

"One of the biggest misconceptions is that re-doing work "slows down" learning for Emily. Ask any artist, novelist, or scientific researcher ~ reworking for better quality results is as important for high-flyers as it is for the struggling student. Redoing work allows students at all levels to stretch their capabilities and deepen their mastery."

STRATEGIES for the First Half

INSTRUCTION

Although teachers are welcome to keep their existing lesson plans for a unit or chapter exactly the same, and simply add a pre-game, half-time, and post-game component to the existing unit lesson plans, some sample strategies for increasing student retention are provided here.

Pairs

Consider using small groups of "pairs" initially in the year. Moving students in and out of pairs creates several advantages for you as the teacher, as well as for student learning:

- It is a simpler process to "chat with a neighbor" for 1-2 minutes, than to orchestrate longer, more involved interactions.

- When working in larger groups (3-4-5) the social dynamics become much more complicated. It's not that you can't, or that you shouldn't. It's more productive to begin with simpler configurations.

- On the down-side, if you have one student doing most of the work in a 4-some, you are 25% efficient. If you have one student doing most of the work in a pairing, you are 50% efficient.

- In pairs, more students have easier access to being heard, to providing ideas and to join in a discussion. (Greenleaf, 1991 and 2005)

Coaching

Based on what you have learned about your students, be sure to honor that for some students mastering this material will take more perseverance, because it is not their natural inclination. EFFORT should always be supported as much as achievement. Reassure the "reluctant learner" that it is your job to nag, nurture, or nudge them toward success, and encourage them to let you play the role of coach: *"Some students have parents who will make them learn this, or make them turn this in, so it is much easier for them to get it done ~let me be that person for you."*

Exemplars

Be sure to provide students with visible, tangible examples of what good work looks like on any particular assignment. They should have those available, and be able to refer to them throughout their own work. It may even be helpful to provide students with examples of NON-quality work as well, as they first learn to be descriptive and specific.

Marzano, Pickering & Pollock's Nine Best Strategies

In an expansive review of the literature, three researchers identified nine of the most effective instructional approaches leading to student achievement (listed in Chapter Six). These strategies, coupled with brain research, have been demonstrated to cause an increase in both initial learning as well as long-term memory. The following three approaches provided are derived from 3 of the 9 strategies.

Categorizing

45% increase: The use of activities that require learners to compare/contrast items and categorize by similarities and differences. Before beginning a new unit, provide students with a host of terms/words that they are likely to be familiar with (randomly written on the board). Ask them, in pairs, to group the terms into categories they believe are appropriate, giving each category they form a "title." After 5 minutes or when done, ask them to offer the categories they generated. These provide potential criteria for how the terms are similar or different. You can then identify and refine (mis)understandings, clarify as needed or frame their thinking with the lesson/unit objective(s) in mind.

Notetaking

34% increase: Summarizing and Note-taking are among the most powerful strategies used that provide opportunities for students to "do the work" of learning. With greater volume of notes a factor, it is also useful to have them revisit notes in conjunction with the social learning system of the brain. To do this, have students reorganize their notes, identifying main ideas and subordinate details. Once they have begun this process, have students work in pairs to compare the items each has selected as important. This causes their brain to review, discuss, and determine where they are with their current thinking. In essence, from the first writing of notes, they have now considered the material up to four times! Similarly, the reluctant learner or the auditory learner who has generated fewer written notes, has an opportunity to listen, reconsider, and to better organize their understanding ~ even if their written results are less extensive.

Predict, Hypothesize, & Test

23% increase: Generating and testing hypotheses. When the mind merely passively listens, it does not need to process as extensively as when we request that a "stand" or position is taken. Now and then, ask learners to *actively* predict something (what happens next, the result of an experiment, the extent of involvement needed to produce an outcome, etc.). Provide a "none-to-all" scale of 1-5 for students to actually circle a response. Ask students to physically get up and stand in a continuum along a wall that depicts their current thinking on an issue. Or perhaps have them create the range of possibilities in outcomes and then sit with a peer who "sees" things differently, to have a discussion of reasons for their views.

Bimodal Approaches

When feasible, consider both visual and verbal (bimodal) facets of an idea, concept or approach. Simply ask students to generate an illustration of a main idea or concept being studied. Or ask them to locate a photograph in a magazine that captures similar meaning. Or have pairs or small groups generate a chart of a key idea that depicts a brief explanation, an illustrative version, similar ideas/processes, and words to help remember the meaning of the key idea. (Greenleaf & Wells-Papanek, 2005)

"Ask the Expert" ~ "Read More About It"

Consider rotating experts for each unit. YOU will create the expert by working with an individual student prior to the classroom work, and providing extra reading and attention. Then, during the unit work, that student has the tools to provide guidance as groups work. You will be surprised at how some of your most reluctant learners blossom, after having been "forced" to become an expert.

Brown Bag Seminars ~ Reading Room

Many students do not have a safe place to study (a place free of distractions and full of support). Consider allowing your classroom to be such a place. Occasionally, host lunchtime chats around an upcoming or concurrent topic. The message you send is two-fold:

1. This will always be an environment where learning is encouraged.

2. Learning can be accomplished and enjoyed through casual conversation.

Step FIVE ~ *The Importance of Half-time*

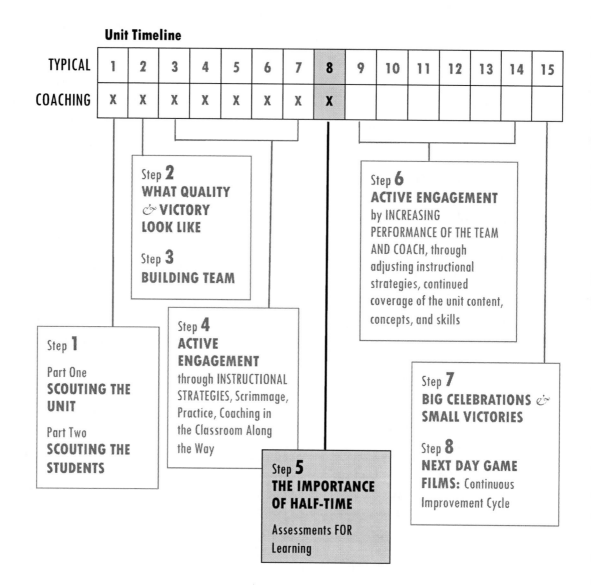

Unit Timeline

	1	2	3	4	5	6	7	8	9	10	11	12	13	14	15
TYPICAL	1	2	3	4	5	6	7	8	9	10	11	12	13	14	15
COACHING	X	X	X	X	X	X	X	X							

Step 2
WHAT QUALITY & VICTORY LOOK LIKE

Step 3
BUILDING TEAM

Step 6
ACTIVE ENGAGEMENT by INCREASING PERFORMANCE OF THE TEAM AND COACH, through adjusting instructional strategies, continued coverage of the unit content, concepts, and skills

Step 1
Part One
SCOUTING THE UNIT
Part Two
SCOUTING THE STUDENTS

Step 4
ACTIVE ENGAGEMENT through INSTRUCTIONAL STRATEGIES, Scrimmage, Practice, Coaching in the Classroom Along the Way

Step 5
THE IMPORTANCE OF HALF-TIME
Assessments FOR Learning

Step 7
BIG CELEBRATIONS & SMALL VICTORIES

Step 8
NEXT DAY GAME FILMS: Continuous Improvement Cycle

OVERVIEW **The Importance of Half-time**

Many of us assume that giving, grading, and handing back results from quizzes and tests IS feedback that helps students do better. Yet most of us readily admit that when we do hand back assignments or exams, students glance at the grade and put it away, or even worse, throw it away. For them, learning over this segment is a done deal. One more portion of the trip over.

RESEARCH ANCHOR

"... standards can be raised only by changes that are put into direct effect by teachers and pupils in classrooms. There is a body of firm evidence that formative assessment is an essential component of classroom work and that its development can raise standards achievement. We know of no other way of raising standards for which such a strong prima facie case can be made."

Black and Wiliam, 1998

It takes more intentionality to truly use assessment for feedback that improves performance. One important part of such formative assessment is the *midway meta-cognition* ~ the old "monitor and adjust." Unfortunately, traditional teaching stuck with the monitoring, but lost sight of making adjustments. Coaching classrooms recognize the value of low-stakes assessment in the learning process. Pick an assignment (or topic, or unit, or project, or standard, etc). So, what's your target goal on the assessment OF learning?? Now... how could you do at least one interim assessment FOR learning, that would help *you* adjust what/how you continue to help THEM adjust their actions? In a low-stakes assessment you are, in effect, grading yourself: *How did I do, in helping all of you to get to the appropriate point, thus far?*

You are also evaluating the effectiveness of the collaborative strategies. It is a time for everyone, including you, to discuss how to change the approach, before continuing on the journey toward mastery.

Mid-course corrections provide opportunities for learning that precede final performance outcomes.

KEY POINT

Three Key Components to a Successful Half-time

1. **The Players** ~ Examine the game so far, and *make adjustments in what the players are doing.* Depending on personal coaching style, these adjustments are sometimes made in low-key, one-on-one ways, or are sometimes a bit more over the top. In both cases, players have no doubt that the message is one aimed at helping them in constructive ways. One way or the other, students are given meaningful feedback and information about what ~ specifically ~ they should begin doing differently, in order to get improved results.

RESEARCH ANCHOR

"Educators who want to ensure student learning must make use of formative assessment and feedback. Formative assessments are standards-based but have as their sole purpose student learning; There are no immediate consequences for poor performance ~ thus no high stakes. These are designed only to support learning."

Danielson, 2002-2003

2. **The Coach** ~ What we often forget is that coaches are also amazingly self-reflective and self-critical, in terms of ownership of the play, so far. They are more than willing to say, "Okay, that game plan I had in the first half isn't working. Instead, let's try..." During a successful half time, both the players *and the coach* are making adjustments.

3. **The Team** ~ How do you keep motivation up for a second half, even if your team is behind? By using those *magic words*: ~ "Hang in there, the game's not over!" The brilliance in a football framework is that half time provides you the ultimate assessment FOR learning. It offers you the ability to examine closely *how the game is going so far,* and to **make adjustments** in the play and the coaching, in order to increase performance in the second half. And, everyone knows the half time score doesn't count. The half time score simply provides you concrete information on where you stand currently, in terms of where you want to be at the end of the game.

Mid-course corrections provide opportunities for learning that precede final performance outcomes. For a number of years, Rick Stiggins has been telling us ~ in different words ~ to embed scrimmage and half time opportunities within our classroom. Low-stakes assessments **for** learning are used to evaluate current performance in order to provide specific feedback on ways to improve, prior to the final assessment **of** learning.

Linking assessment to instruction, W. James Popham writes "...the array of test-like events in assessment *for* learning is always linked to the question. 'What's next instructionally?'" (Popham, 2006)

Jay McTighe and Ken O'Connor have long told us that the best teachers recognize assessment as an ongoing and concurrent classroom tool, and use it to adjust their practice and guide their students to improve. In the November, 2005 issue of Educational Leadership, they identified seven practices that will help students achieve maximum performance, which we have embedded in the coaching framework:

Pre-Game Preparation

1. Showing students a meaningful performance assessment at the beginning of any new unit.
2. Showing criteria and models in advance, to help students have a clear conception of what is meant by "quality work."
3. Assessing before teaching, to determine where students are.
4. Offering appropriate choices.

On-The-Field and In-The-Game

5. Providing feedback early and often.

6. Encouraging self-assessment and interim goal setting.

Post-Game Celebrations and Reflections

7. Allowing new evidence of achievement to replace old evidence.

RESEARCH ANCHOR

"When anyone is trying to learn, feedback about the effort has three elements: redefinition of the *desired goal*, evidence about *present position*, and some understanding of a *way to close the gap between the two*. All three must be understood to some degree by anyone before he or she can take action to improve learning."

Black and Wiliam, 1998

The main point of embedding a "half-time" opportunity within the unit is so that students can again have an opportunity to participate in the thinking and working that goes into continuous improvement. Involving students in a reflection of their work so far and in designing a plan for improvement prior to evaluation requires students to experiment, observe, and draw inferences about what does and doesn't work. As they summarize conclusions to share with the team, and shape those ideas into classroom applications for the second half, they approach the rest of the unit with a greater sense of confidence, and the willingness to continue to rise to the challenges ahead.

Rick Stiggins notes that in assessments **for** learning, "Students partner with their teacher to continuously monitor their current level of attainment in relation to agreed-upon expectations so they can set goals for what to learn next and thus play a role in communicating evidence of learning to one another, to their teacher, to their families, and they do so not just after learning has been completed but all along the journey to success." (Stiggins, 2005)

This sounds logical, and not that hard to do, but ~ in fact ~ it is a cultural shift from school as usual. Although half-time is an invitation for students and the teacher to embark on a new and better pathway for the second half, it requires a "bravery" on the part of the teacher as coach, that that is captured below.

> "Rarely, if ever, did they [teachers] say to their classes, 'This just isn't working. I can see that most of you aren't learning much ~ are you? Please tell me if I'm exaggerating the problem. But as I see it, whatever we're trying to accomplish, we're obviously not doing it very well. We need to rethink what we're doing. If you aren't learning much; if you're not engaged, not desirous of learning more about this topic, then obviously we're on the wrong track, and we should be doing something quite, quite different." (Fried, 2005)

Coaches recognize that a statement like the one above is not an admission of inadequacy, but rather a key, mid-game strategy that speaks to the wisdom of coaching for increased performance. It is in the mutual responsibility and the mutual adjustments, that brains and hearts are recaptured.

The assessments FOR learning embedded in the coaching framework give renewed hope to the "Jasons" in the room, who are accustomed to having past poor performance hobble any enthusiasm or motivation to engage in future work. It is this "opening up" of the mind that now invites reluctant learners to engage as they begin to more clearly understand the learning goal and know how they will be evaluated; when they come to believe the learning goals and assessments are meaningful, and worth learning; and when they come to believe in their potential for ultimate success, within this supportive framework.

Research & RESULTS

Mid-Course Assessment & Feedback

Black and Wiliam, 1998   In a review of over twenty studies, ranging over age groups from 5-year-olds to university undergraduates, across several school subjects, and over several countries ~ *all* showed that the strengthening of the practice of formative [mid-course] assessment produced significant and often substantial learning gains. Furthermore, Black and Wiliam reported that improved [intermittent] formative assessment helps low achievers more than other students and so reduces the range of achievement [gap] while raising achievement overall.

Marzano, Pickering & Pollock, 2001   One of the best uses of feedback to learners is to explain what is accurate and what is inaccurate at intermittent and/or crucial, transitional times.

Reeves, 1990   "… schools with significant improvements [in student achievement outcomes] provided significantly more frequent feedback to students… in real-time."

STRATEGIES for Half-Time

Obstacle Course

As soon as the grading period reports have been distributed, have students analyze their successes and failures, looking for obstacles within (time management, skill weakness, character trait) and without (friends, teachers, parents, job). Develop strategy plans for overcoming obstacles. Determine which peers, adults, and places can help them develop better study habits. Detail how to put a new study plan into action. Plan an immediate reward for getting past the first hurdle. Some classes literally have students design and post a visual representation of the academic goal with the obstacles in the path, and move the "player" through the course, celebrating each small victory. Teachers can have students calculate their grade point averages overall, and within each unit. Students can predict certain grades on assignments and in classes during the next grading period, and see how averages would change.

"Mission Accomplished" ~ Evidentiary Hearings

One step is to simply ask what, or how, a student is doing. *A much more important step is that each student be able to prove it!* Helping students learn to collect evidence of their work efforts will build their own sense of confidence, as well as impact their academic achievement.

Students should be involved in developing their own scoring guides as often as possible. This helps students develop an understanding of the components involved in successful completion of assignments, and activities. As students bring up goals and assignments, teams could develop rubrics or checklists that help them measure how well and how much they have accomplished.

One way to get students to understand the concept of providing specific detail and producing artifacts is to hold "Evidentiary Hearings," where students have to *prove*, through product and detail, how they have successfully completed a class assignment, or mastered a core standard. Students can role-play mock court situations, as they examine the evidence in each unit, or assessment activity.

Half-Time in the Locker Room

Classes using a sports theme can relate midway meta-cognition activities to how sports teams use half time to rethink their "game plan," and make

adjustments in the second half. Every student sets a concrete unit goal. At the midway point, students write a two-paragraph essay. In the first paragraph, they write about what worked for them and did not work for them (both in terms of what they did, and what YOU did) as they worked on their goal. In paragraph two, they write about changes in their game plan, and recommend changes in your "coaching" in the second half. At the end of the unit, a debriefing essay is a comparison and analysis on whether more was accomplished the second half.

Organizational Skills Templates

At "half-time" or other intervals in the unit, provide students with an organizational template that requests them to use what they know to create pro/con or for/against lists of information. For instance, if you were studying the French Revolution, you might ask them to make two lists, one of things causing the revolution to come about and one of things that might have delayed or deterred people from revolting at that time. It is at this time that you can walk about and quickly get a sense of what level of understanding each student has. Perhaps, this may guide some discussion to help those who are still struggling… and reinforce those who seem to be on track. Once they have either worked on this for homework or in-class, have them meet in pairs to discuss each other's ideas. Expand the pairs to quads or a whole class discussion as you wish.

Maps

Bimodal exercises that employ both visual and verbal modes of representation are not only effective for processing and for memory they are also efficient ways to gather feedback on how students are doing. Provide a blank outline of the landform of a country. Ask learners to track the movement of the military, the migration of people, the explorer's route, etc. as it aligns with the unit. They could do this every 2-3 days, keeping pace with the knowledge of the unit. At any point while they are working on their "map," you can move about, glance, and see how their learning is portrayed in this representational form. It will be quite clear who needs additional assistance! This could also be altered somewhat and done with a procedure, a process or a chronology for a story.

Peer Feedback

Have students exchange papers (a piece of work completed to that point in time). Ask them to use the scoring rubric to assess the work they are looking at and to provide their peer with some feedback about (1) why they rated the work as they did and (2) one thing they might address that would greatly advance the quality of it. By looking over the FEEDBACK provided, you get a clear picture of what the learner understands.

Photo Pre-Finish

Take a photograph from the chapter or that relates to a main topic in your unit. Ask students to write three important things that they glean from the picture. This will inform you about their current thinking and depth of understanding. Next, have students work in pairs to prioritize the top two most important items to be derived from the image.

The Actual Test

Let's return to the classroom where a teacher had used "the actual test" during pre-game preparation (p. 40). Take a quick guess at what she used for her half-time assessment for learning. As you recall, students had posted three charts on the wall: one identifying terms they would need to know, one identifying concepts they would need to know, and one identifying what a high quality, open-response answer would look like. They checked off progress on these charts along the way, during the first half.

Instead of creating a separate midway assessment, the teacher simply gives them ~ again ~ the end of unit, rigorous, open-response exam, where questions required high-level interpretation, and answers required depth and detail.

The midway meta-cognition became an analysis of whether or not they had "correctly" marked off the terms and concepts they knew, and which ones they would need to go back and revisit. Students who did well on certain questions were paired with students who had struggled with that question, and pairs identified where the gaps were.

Most importantly, students had a chance to check the quality of their answers, and determine which of the criteria were lacking in a high-level, in-depth, specific response.

Students constructed a new team goal and talked about strategies for the second half, now feeling much more confident in how their final assessment would turn out.

Chemical Talk

When applicable, have students create a conversation that the "components" under study might have. A chemistry teacher could ask students to create a dialogue between the elements that characterizes oxidation. A math teacher could ask learners to generate dialogue between the two sides of the equation (opposite the "=" sign). A casual look at the created communications will tell you leagues about the understanding of the students.

The 50/50 Split

Even when you encounter an academic or behavioral situation with an individual student, it is important to allow that student some choices in how to proceed. One effective tool is the 50/50 split ~ "I will own half of this problem and contribute to the solution, if you will also own half and contribute to the solution." (Template follows)

The 50/50 **SPLIT**

Learning or Growth Experience _____

By entering this agreement, we will each take part in the journey, contributing to success in the following manner:

STUDENT PART

Name _____

TEACHER PART

Name _____

What is the goal or objective to be achieved? What needs to be done?

Student _____

_____

_____

_____

Teacher _____

_____

_____

_____

How is it going to happen? Brainstorm some activities or strategies that could help make this happen. List some specific resources within/outside the school that could help.

Student Tasks To Do?	Completion Date	Teacher Tasks To Do?	Completion Date

How are we going to prove that we did our part and accomplished the goals? Evidence and Verification:

Student _____

_____

Teacher _____

_____

How well was each task completed? Who will provide feedback about the progress or quality of the work?

Student _____

_____

Teacher _____

_____

We agree to meet and either celebrate or renegotiate on: _____ Date

Date _____ Student Signature _____   Teacher Signature _____

Donegan, Greenleaf, and Wells-Papanek, 2006

Step SIX ~ *Increased Performance in the Second Half*

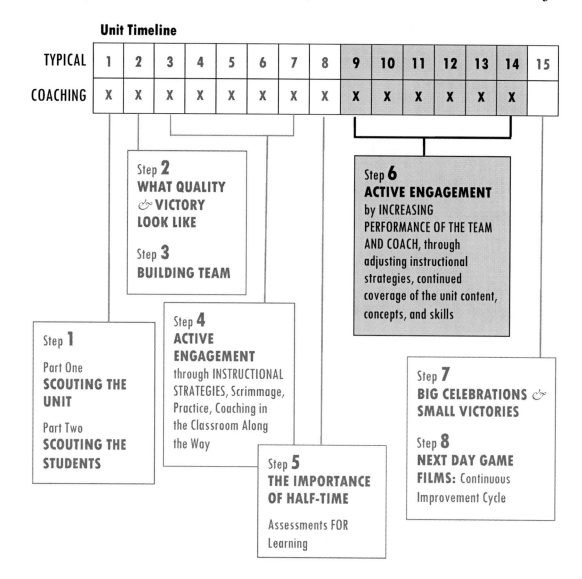

Unit Timeline

TYPICAL	1	2	3	4	5	6	7	8	9	10	11	12	13	14	15
COACHING	X	X	X	X	X	X	X	X	X	X	X	X	X	X	

Step 2
WHAT QUALITY
& **VICTORY**
LOOK LIKE

Step 3
BUILDING TEAM

Step 6
ACTIVE ENGAGEMENT
by INCREASING
PERFORMANCE OF THE TEAM
AND COACH, through
adjusting instructional
strategies, continued
coverage of the unit content,
concepts, and skills

Step 1
Part One
SCOUTING THE
UNIT
Part Two
SCOUTING THE
STUDENTS

Step 4
ACTIVE
ENGAGEMENT
through INSTRUCTIONAL
STRATEGIES, Scrimmage,
Practice, Coaching in
the Classroom Along
the Way

Step 7
BIG CELEBRATIONS *&*
SMALL VICTORIES

Step 8
NEXT DAY GAME
FILMS: Continuous
Improvement Cycle

Step 5
THE IMPORTANCE
OF HALF-TIME
Assessments FOR
Learning

OVERVIEW **Increased Performance in the Second Half**

Do not assume you can simply retake the field, with players that are now
entirely self-motivated and knowledgeable about what it takes to win. *It is here
that the traditional classroom frequently loses a number of players altogether.* In
the second half, the cycle of coaching, practice, coaching, scrimmage, coaching
continues. What you should be seeing in the remainder of the unit, however, are
players with new insight, and renewed work ethic.

Teaching is about making adjustments, as they relate to the results.

Research & **RESULTS**

Mid Course Instructional Adjustments

Assessment Practice

Reeves, 2003

"The consistent message of 90/90/90 schools is that the penalty for poor performance is not a low grade, followed by a forced march to the next unit. Rather, student performance that is less than proficient is followed by multiple opportunities to improve performance." "Most of the schools conducted weekly assessments of student progress… these assessments were not district or state tests, but were assessments constructed and administered by classroom teachers. The consequence of students performing badly was not an admonishment to 'Wait until next year' but rather the promise that 'You can do better next week.'"

"In fact, when students know that there are not additional opportunities to succeed, they frequently take teacher feedback on their performance and stuff it into desks, back packs, and wastebaskets. Students in this scenario are happy with a 'D' and unmotivated by an 'F'."

"In a classroom assessment scenario in which there are multiple opportunities to improve, however, the consequence for poor performance is not a bad grade and discouragement, but more work, improved performance, and respect for teacher feedback."

Implications for Assessment Practices

Guskey, NCA 2004

#1: Assessments must be a source of information for both students and teachers (no surprises embedded).

#2: Assessments need to be followed by high quality corrective instruction.

#3: Students must be given a second chance to show improvement.

Step SIX ~ Increased Performance in the Second Half *Checklist for Success*

Questions I should **ask myself** *during* each "unit":

Questions I must **ask the kids** along the way *(knowing I may need to coach them to correct answers)*:

☐ **Overriding "Quality Check" Question: Who's doing the work here: me? or the kids?**

☐ Have they revisited the <u>ending assessment</u> at this point in the unit?

☐ How is the class doing on the "performance goal" set at the beginning?

☐ Is the charted progress posted? Is there a "visual" for the individual and class?

☐ Have I made adjustments based on the <u>assessment FOR learning...</u> and strategized about it WITH the kids?

☐ Is there clear, sufficient cause for a mini-<u>celebration regarding progress at this time</u>?

☐ What now looks hardest and why?

☐ What adjustments do we need to make to help each other learn the material?

☐ What kind of support is needed at this time?

☐ How can we make it more interesting?

☐ How are we doing with the upcoming "proof" that we have learned it?

☐ **How's it going so far?** What should we change?

☐ What are the best and most important parts so far?

☐ What would increase performance at this time?

In our coaching framework, Post-Game Reflections contains:

Post-Game Reflections   page 97   **Step SEVEN**
Big Celebrations and Small Victories

    page 99   **Step EIGHT**
Next Day Game Films

Step SEVEN ~ *Post-Game Reflections*

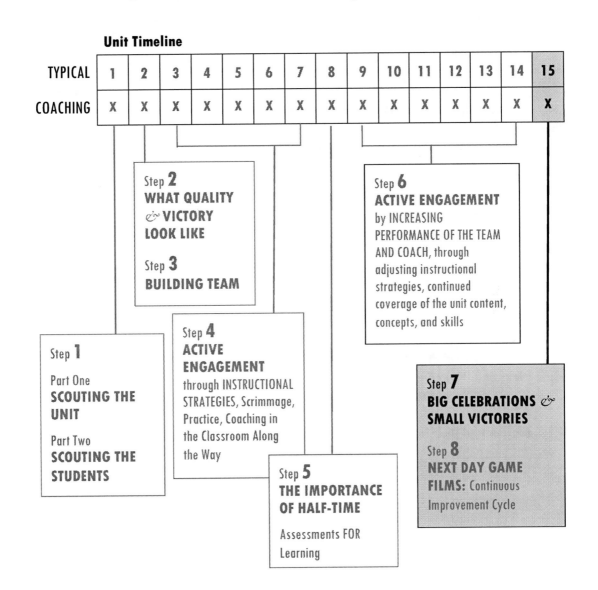

Unit Timeline

	1	2	3	4	5	6	7	8	9	10	11	12	13	14	15
TYPICAL	1	2	3	4	5	6	7	8	9	10	11	12	13	14	15
COACHING	X	X	X	X	X	X	X	X	X	X	X	X	X	X	X

Step **2**
WHAT QUALITY
& **VICTORY**
LOOK LIKE

Step **3**
BUILDING TEAM

Step **6**
ACTIVE ENGAGEMENT
by INCREASING
PERFORMANCE OF THE TEAM
AND COACH, through
adjusting instructional
strategies, continued
coverage of the unit content,
concepts, and skills

Step **1**
Part One
**SCOUTING THE
UNIT**
Part Two
**SCOUTING THE
STUDENTS**

Step **4**
**ACTIVE
ENGAGEMENT**
through INSTRUCTIONAL
STRATEGIES, Scrimmage,
Practice, Coaching in
the Classroom Along
the Way

Step **5**
**THE IMPORTANCE
OF HALF-TIME**
Assessments FOR
Learning

Step **7**
BIG CELEBRATIONS *&*
SMALL VICTORIES

Step **8**
**NEXT DAY GAME
FILMS:** Continuous
Improvement Cycle

RESEARCH ANCHOR

"Students benefit from assessment **FOR** learning in several critical ways. First, they become more confident learners because they get to watch themselves succeeding. This success permits them to take the risk of continuing to try to learn. The result is greater achievement for all students ~ especially low achievers, which helps reduce the achievement gap between middle-class and low-socioeconomic-status students."

Stiggins, 2002

RESEARCH ANCHOR

"...[Assessment/feedback strategies used to] *build students' confidence* in themselves as learners and help them take responsibility for their own learning... [will help to] lay a foundation for lifelong learning." [Similarly,] Actively involving students in communicating with their teacher and their families about their achievement status and improvement [is important].

Stiggins, 2002

Big Celebrations and Small Victories

In "big-time" high school football, it is not unusual for teams to travel hundreds of miles to play a Friday night game, where they get trounced by the opposing team. Back in the locker room, they have ten minutes to get out of uniform and onto the bus, to make the lonely ride home in the dark, exhausted and depressed. Any coach worth his salt will tell you that this ten minute transition is not the time to raise a ruckus about what went wrong. Instead, the coach tries to point out tiny victories. "Hey, Kevin, great catch in the third quarter. We're gonna need more of that next week." "Reynaldo, can we expect some more sacks like that last one? You sure caught him by surprise!" Although it doesn't do a great deal to change the mood on the bus, it reminds them that not everything is bleak. There are sparks of talent, sparks of brilliance... to be rekindled next week.

Always be sure to celebrate small successes by individuals and the class, along the way. You don't have to pass kids just because they try hard, but you do need to recognize and articulate their incremental improvement and work efforts. In classroom units, not every individual will reach his or her goal on the final assessment. It becomes an important coaching role for the teacher to work with students to help them identify the tiny moments when they mastered a skill, or retained a piece of the puzzle ~ to help them find moments to build on, noting what worked, and to remind them to hang in there because, "there's another game next week."

On the other hand, nothing is more fun than celebrating with a team and coach that cares about you, when you win the game. Having set a team performance goal on the unit, and reaching that goal is cause for celebration, and taking the time to celebrate creates momentum that will carry over into the next unit.

Step **EIGHT** ~ *Next Day Game Films*

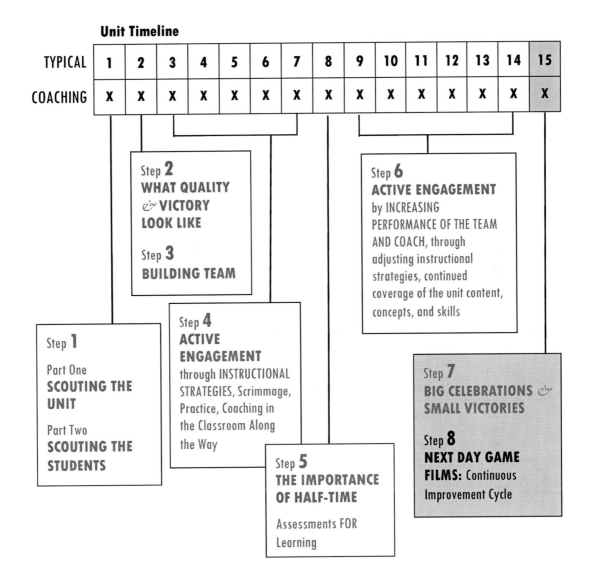

Unit Timeline

TYPICAL	1	2	3	4	5	6	7	8	9	10	11	12	13	14	15
COACHING	x	x	x	x	x	x	x	x	x	x	x	x	x	x	x

Step **2**
WHAT QUALITY & VICTORY LOOK LIKE

Step **3**
BUILDING TEAM

Step **6**
ACTIVE ENGAGEMENT by INCREASING PERFORMANCE OF THE TEAM AND COACH, through adjusting instructional strategies, continued coverage of the unit content, concepts, and skills

Step **1**
Part One **SCOUTING THE UNIT**
Part Two **SCOUTING THE STUDENTS**

Step **4**
ACTIVE ENGAGEMENT through INSTRUCTIONAL STRATEGIES, Scrimmage, Practice, Coaching in the Classroom Along the Way

Step **7**
BIG CELEBRATIONS & SMALL VICTORIES

Step **8**
NEXT DAY GAME FILMS: Continuous Improvement Cycle

Step **5**
THE IMPORTANCE OF HALF-TIME
Assessments FOR Learning

OVERVIEW **The Continuous Improvement Cycle**

However supportive the coach might have been on the ride home Friday night, Saturday morning is another story. In field houses around the country, Saturday morning finds coaches watching the game films carefully and repeatedly. They then involve the whole team in watching honestly and critically the previous performance, with one clear question foremost on their mind, "How do we get better?" What went right, and how do we take that skill forward? What went wrong, and what practice and coaching will improve it?

Who needs to do what? How do we help ourselves get better? How do we help each other get better? And how do we take what we have learned into the next game? What should our personal goal and our team goal be for next week?

The cycle continues ~ with the next unit's pre-game preparation now building on past experiences. Support for improved performance is built into the coaching framework. All the professional development, in-service speakers in the world can't provide the same insight and information, as the coaching conversations held in post-game reflections.

The focus of the coaching framework is to create a classroom culture dedicated to continuous improvement through a sense of shared responsibility for reaching the common goal.

Barbara Given tells us, from a brain and learning vantage point that much of what goes into the learning process is carried forward to new experiences. "The reflective learning system... relies on prior experience and knowledge as it integrates new learning. Without activating this system, the other four systems [of the brain] can produce only limited results. This refers to the personal consideration of one's own learning... achievements, failures, what worked, what didn't and what needs improvement." She continues, in talking about how learners benefit from understanding themselves and their approaches to learning that, "Knowledge of one's individual learning style, and learning how to use style preferences can produce great academic gain. Without explicit instruction in self-monitoring and performance analysis, [learning behaviors] can go dreadfully underdeveloped." We need to teach students reflective thinking and meta-cognition deliberately, in a consistent manner, until students internalize the process."

Post game activities serve to build on past experiences and increase the probability of successes in the tomorrow's to come. Similarly, the act of establishing the end of unit summative assessment *before* instruction begins serves to identify learning targets for the students. Once known, the student can better determine how to go about mastering the essentials of the knowledge and skills ahead. This success permits them to take the risk of continuing to try to learn. The result is greater achievement for all students ~ especially low achievers, which helps reduce the achievement gap between middle-class and low-socioeconomic-status students." Thus, the creation of a final, summative measure(s) in the beginning ~ and the ultimate administering of the end of unit assessment ~ establish clear, articulated "bookends" that learners can rely upon to chart their course.

STRATEGIES for the Post-Game

Score!

At the end of each unit (or timeframe), be sure to celebrate the improvements made by individuals and the accomplishment of overall goals Some teachers post goals and have a visual representation for noting success, such as a staircase, football field with gridlines, racetrack, or the traditional chart with stars. Some departments have competitions between classes, and the class that gained the most "yardage" (the most students achieved their goal) is recognized on school announcements. Additional communication practice occurs when these classes come together, and challenge each other in Evidentiary Hearings.

Evaluation Forms

Make sure to provide an avenue for collecting individual student's opinions on *"How's it going?"* ~ for them, and for you. Not only does it continue to provide you with important information, it can also help reinforce for the student what they have accomplished.

Four-Two-Two Evaluations ~ Have each student write down "the **four** most important things they have learned" today, this week, this topic, or this unit. Then pair them up. Look at what the two of them have written and then decide what are the **two** most important things they have learned this _____. Then mix the pairs, forming new pairs and have them prioritize the top 2 most important things they have learned. How do they feel?

Some teachers have students do a daily reflection on how it is going, what they need, etc. on an index card or in a journal.

Student Led Conferences ~ Portfolio

One of the strongest components of post-game is the reflections. This is where students step back and look at their learning. They talk about what's working for them, and where they can apply the strategies that they are learning. One excellent way to promote ownership in ongoing personal progress is through the use of portfolios, involving students in the periodic oral presentation of their personal progress, and their plan for improvement. These strategies provide students and teachers with tools and artifacts that build student accountability and ownership in their academic progress. Take time to look at sample reflection and progress forms used in portfolios and student-led conferences available from reliable sources.

Analyze This! Designers Challenge ~ Case Studies

Debriefing done with each unit about personal and class successes, and subsequent revisions, can also be used to address your content goals for each student. Some teachers refer to it as "Designer's Challenge." Have a student who did not meet his goal volunteer to be the Case Study/Client. Students work in teams to discuss strategies that this student could use in overcoming particular obstacles that kept him from succeeding. They could design concrete plans for the following week, to meet his particular academic goal. Students practice working in teams, present their action plans, and the volunteer selects a plan to adopt and put into practice the following week. The individual student benefits not only from the new plan of action, but also from whole-group support and monitoring throughout the next week. *In addition, the other students also wind up applying what they just discussed to their own goal setting for the upcoming unit.*

Rising Star Honor Roll

Coaching classrooms should be keenly aware of small incremental improvements, and celebrate those small successes with their students as often as possible. It is this reinforcement that builds a cycle of success, and will eventually promote larger goals and self-motivation. One excellent activity can be done within each class grading period or, better yet, for each unit. It is fine to have an "A" honor roll and a "B" honor roll, and many classes have reward systems in place for students on those rolls. Now, switch to a Rising Star Honor Roll, posted just as prominently. Any student who has increased their grade point from the previous grading period, or any student who has improved from pre-test to post-test on a unit, is posted alphabetically on this roll. Since all students' names will qualify for this honor roll, there is no weighted stigma attached, and no one knows whether you have qualified because you have gone from a 92 to a 96, or a 52 to a 66. Do not make underperforming students wait until they have an A or B average to be recognized for their improvements.

IN SUMMARY We began this chapter with a comparison between two teachers in a hypothetical 15-day unit. One succumbs to the high-pressure, high-speed coverage model, and barely stops to catch her breath in the mere fifteen days she was allotted for this unit. She started out on day one, stuck to the route prescribed, and pulled back into the driveway on schedule. She tried her best from the front seat to explain why the trip was important and make it interesting. Every moment of every day, she worked hard to ensure that all the content in the unit was delivered, assignments were handed out, activities were completed, assessments were given, and graded. The Emilys did just fine.

Our second teacher, even though he had to stick to the same schedule, did not stick to the same game plan. He made fewer stops, but at the most important places, for longer amounts of time. He spent time in the beginning involving students in "conversations" about how to identify the power standards within the unit, how to make them relevant, and even how to make them interesting. He involved them in the beginning in how they could prove they learned the important stuff, what the assessment would look like, and what quality work would look like. Together, they set a goal for what they wanted to "get" out of this unit ~ for life, for learning, and for the test.

RESEARCH ANCHOR

"We need to teach students reflective thinking and meta-cognition deliberately, in a consistent manner, until students internalize the process."

Given, 2002

Halfway through, they checked on how the trip was going so far. They tested themselves on the goals they had set, and strategized together about how each individual could improve, the teacher could improve, and how they could *all* **help each other** do that.

In the end, when tested, there was time to reflect. What had they learned that was important ~ from the unit? from the experience? from the teacher? from themselves? A cycle of continuous improvement, a culture of "learning and thinking about thinking and learning," a TEAM where all worked together on important and challenging matters, was created. Celebrations were due!

Look at the "scoreboard" illustration on page 99. A casual glance will create the appearance that four days were "lost" (to scouting, teamwork, half-time formative assessments, and post-game).

In reality, it is those four days in which the brains and hearts of reluctant learners are found, reeled in, and ultimately captured. It is in the foreshadowing of the learning in the unit, the midway meta-cognition about the learning in the unit, and the reflection and celebration of the learning at the end of the unit ~ that retention and application is accomplished.

It is a slower, and more satisfying way to teach; it is a deeper, and more complex way to teach; and it is a more successful way to teach. In a coaching classroom with power standards teaching, the entire range of students, from Emily to Jason, will do better on the end of unit exam, the end of course exam, on state assessments, and ~ most importantly ~ in the long-term, personal application. Way to go, coach!

Research & **Results**

Post-Learning Reflective Assessment

McTighe and Thomas, 2003

There are three stages to the process of assessing learners:

First   Determine student-learning goals

Second   Collect, analyze and interpret evidence from multiple sources of data to determine how students are doing

Third   Consider the root causes of present achievement levels and then ~ and only then ~ implement systematic actions to address root causes, promote enduring learning, and increase test scores.

McCombs, 2002

"In Learner-centered principles, "Practices integrate learning and motivational strategies to help students become self-directed learners."

Greenleaf, "*Creating and Changing Mindsets*," 2005

"Research indicates that even a child who does not believe in her/himself will succeed… if s/he has two adults in her/his life who do believe in her/him (and express it). There is something magical about another human being demonstrating a complete faith in who we are and what we are capable of accomplishing."

Step EIGHT ~ **Next Day Game Films** *Checklist for Success*

Questions I should **ask myself** *after each "unit":*	Questions I must **ask the kids** *after the unit:*
☐ **Overriding "Quality Check" Question: Who did the work here: me? or the kids?**	☐ Were we correct about what was important?
☐ Did every student attain the <u>POWER standards</u>?	☐ Were we correct about what was hardest?
☐ Did the class meet the "performance goal" as a team?	☐ What best related to "real" life?
☐ Was the charting of progress helpful along the way?	☐ What approaches were most successful to help us (me) learn?
☐ Did the <u>assessment FOR learning</u> and adjusted strategies work?	☐ How can we "prove" we learned it?
☐ Did the <u>non-compliers</u> improve in the second half?	☐ Did we achieve quality?
☐ Was there <u>celebration, reflection, and revision</u> at the end of the unit?	☐ What were the best and most important parts of the unit?
	☐ What would increase performance in the next unit?

We have talked a lot inside the coaching framework about the vital and "nontraditional" role of assessment. Perhaps the hallmark of all great coaches is the same message sent to Michael Lewis by Coach Fitz, the ability to convey *"such confident trust in my ability that I had no choice but to live up to it."* **Failure was NOT an option.**

Chapter **FOUR** *Failure is* **NOT an Option.**

OVERVIEW

Remember Emily and Jason? Ever since elementary school, Emily has been a quick learner. She consistently scored high on tests and got great report card grades. As a result, she became increasingly confident and continues to believe success is within her reach. On the other hand, Jason didn't fare so well. Beginning in the earliest grades, he began scoring low on tests and thus began questioning his capability to learn. He began to lose confidence and quickly decided it was better not to try and thus save face. By the time they both arrive in our classroom, they enter a high school culture that says, "It's your responsibility to take advantage of the opportunity to learn. If you give up and stop trying, that's your problem, not the teacher's or the school's." Jason's done for.

As we invest in a coaching classroom framework, it is also prudent to examine school and classroom policies that impact student achievement outcomes. We need to ensure that our practices are aligned to send consistent messages of encouragement and high expectations for our learners. Two such practices (among others) would be those of grading and homework.

Within school as usual, there are traditional grading practices that become obstacles to engaging the brains and hearts of today's students. The coaching framework can have more success with more students, **if** classrooms *also* employ grading practices that are compatible with the goal of a coaching classroom: SUCCESS IS THE ONLY OPTION. The role of the teacher in a coaching classroom is not only to assume all students can achieve a viable level of academic success, but also to coach all students to believe this of themselves.

In *Telling Stories of Change*, McCombs quotes a student saying:

> *"This class, it's challenging. It's challenging, but it's not one of the ones where you say, 'Oh God, I'm not going to pass.' This teacher helps you out to where he makes sure you don't fail... 'Cause that's what Mr. McDonald first said when we first got here. 'Nobody is going to fail this class. Nobody...' Now we just come in here and quit talking - we want to get to work."*

If this seems overly optimistic, that is exactly the point. It is the "expected" success that is the hallmark of a coaching classroom. In *Creating and Changing Mindsets*, one strategy is the "as-if" action. This strategy suggests that when we approach a learner "as-if" s/he were capable, instead of having expectations based out of their past behavior patterns, they will rise to the challenge. (Greenleaf, 2005)

In contrast, a surprising number of today's students say that teachers expect them to fail, or at least expect a portion of their class to fail. Students normally have two responses to grading assessments ~ optimistic or pessimistic. Stiggins points out that "An optimistic response leaves learners ready to keep trying and knowing what to do next: students maintain their desire to achieve and press on. A pessimistic response leaves learners feeling that the target remains beyond reach: students stop trying." Through coaching, teachers provide the scaffolding that enables students to respond optimistically: clear individual and team goals, examples of and input on "quality," continuous feedback, opportunities to improve *before* the final grade, and support to insist they climb the scaffold.

Frustrated by low-performing students, traditional teachers frequently resort to the coercion of low grades or failure, and then get even more frustrated when it doesn't work. Fear of failure creates negative stress that causes many of today's students to disengage or shut down. As discussed earlier, the unique job description held by a coaching teacher is, "all children can learn, and it's my job to see that they do." Perhaps the additional message in that statement is, "You can relax now. You WILL succeed." When students come to believe that the team and the coach will "stick with them" in overcoming obstacles and conquering challenges; when they learn that it is **where they arrive** that counts, not when they arrive or where they have been ~ optimism gradually overtakes pessimism as the dominant perspective. Students who don't fear failure can take risks that propel them to higher levels of achievement.

Regardless of how much research points out the ineffectiveness of our current standard grading system, schools remain dominated by testing and grading practices that are counterproductive to the relationships needed between teachers and students to increase work ethic and performance. Most of us are stuck with the prevailing model that results in students who give the teacher the minimum effort required for whichever grade they seek. As Robert Fried points out, "the price we pay for clinging to yesterday's grading practices is that few students bother to show us their best stuff."

GRADES AND PERFORMANCE

Three prominent educational researchers have focused on the need to reexamine how we grade and how we use grades to increase student performance. Their synthesized positions follow:

Stiggins, 1998

The critical emotions underpinning the decision-making process include anxiety, fear of failure, uncertainty, and unwillingness to take risks ~ all triggered by students' perceptions of their own capabilities as reflected in assessment results. Some students responded to the demands of such environments by working hard and learning a great deal. Others controlled their anxiety by giving up and not caring. The result for them? Exactly the opposite of the one society wants. Instead of leaving no child behind, these practices, in effect, drove down the achievement of at least as many students as they successfully elevated.

Fried, 2001

Everything students do in school is calculated as a function of time spent and grades received. Yet time and grades are about the worst incentives we could devise for getting students to think hard and produce work of high quality. As motivators of excellence, grades are awful. Almost nothing in life gets graded. Eggs, maybe. There is hardly a non-school learning program that relies on letter grades or time spent as measures of learning achievement. Every corporation, agency, or organization that trains its own employees ~ from McDonald's and Xerox, to teaching hospitals, to the U.S. Army ~ has developed a far more accurate and purposeful measure of learner achievement: it's called performance, and it is aimed at producing quality.

Teachers on the other hand, get snared by a line of reasoning that goes something like this...

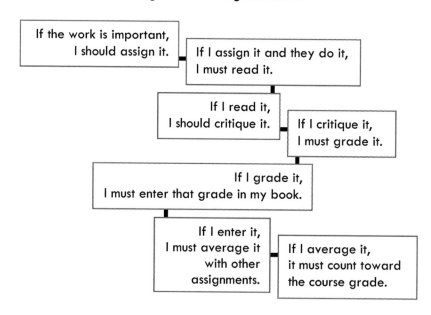

Glasser, 1998 As the record clearly shows, current grading practices don't work. Despite being threatened or punished, over half the students who attend public schools do very little. They don't believe that making much effort in school is worth it…What we lack is not more information from tests or other sources. It is the will to abandon our traditional "teach, test, rank, and coerce the losers" system of education, which, at best, does not work for more than half the students.

The irony is that the very grading practices we use result in fewer students being willing to work hard at something until they get it.

RESEARCH ANCHOR

"Marking is usually conscientious but often fails to offer guidance on how work can be improved. It a significant minority of cases, marking reinforces underachievement and under-expectation by being too generous or unfocused. Information about pupil performance received by the teacher is insufficiently used to inform subsequent work."

Black and Wiliam, 1998

In a coaching classroom students begin to take pride in setting and reaching high standards. A coaching framework allows you to embrace a new way of looking at grading practices and homework policies where students feel better and perform better.

Even though many teachers, as well as students, would like to break away from the paradigm of current use of assessments and grades, we worry about how else we could get kids to turn things in or do them correctly. It is in the coaching framework that students begin to take pride in setting and reaching high standards of performance.

A coaching framework allows you to embrace a new way of looking at grading practices and homework policies where students feel better and perform better.

KEY POINT

Extrinsic vs. Intrinsic Motivation

When a sense of purpose is identified and initiated from within, far less push is needed from without.

In a coaching classroom, teachers really begin thinking deeply about what they want their students to **feel**, *as well as* what they want them to know and how they want them to behave. They no longer chase top-down, compliance-based strategies but rather begin exploring new ways of thinking that create optimistic, even joyful, options.

"Traditionally, schools have used assessment ~ the pending final exam, the unannounced pop quiz, and the threat of low or failing report card grades ~ to motivate students. To maximize learning, our teachers believed, maximize anxiety. Assessment has served as the great intimidator. Pressure to get high test scores and good grades, it was believed, would motivate greater effort and thus more learning." (Glasser, 1999)

What we know, of course, is that only works for Emily. And even with the Emilys, extrinsic motivation is short-lived and liable to quickly dissipate when the external motivator is gone. When the reward or punishment is withdrawn, high-level performance also tends to disappear. External motivators can rob students of their natural desire to learn and do well. In *The Game of School*, Fried states that the case against most existing grading systems is that they hurt kids ~ highly-motivated students like Emily, as well as underperforming students like Jason. **The grade and not learning becomes the goal.** "If the grade is the prize and the teacher is the giver of grades, then pleasing or 'psyching out' the teacher becomes the focus of the students' actions." (Fried, 2005) We want grades to build responsibility, but the problem with extrinsic motivation is that teachers own the accomplishments even more than the students do. Coaching classrooms support *intrinsic* motivation.

> ### RESEARCH ANCHOR
>
> **Research on learner efficacy [belief in capability to succeed] stipulates that a learner needs to believe that they can, given reasonable effort, succeed at a task. "When intrinsically motivated, students tend to employ strategies that demand more effort and that enable them to process information more deeply."**
>
> **Lepper, 1988**

For students to own their accomplishments, they must become intrinsically motivated to do high-level work. Converting from external to internal motivators is not easy. Hard work is not its own reward. Hard work is hard work. The reward comes at the end of hard work, when success is finally achieved. The role of the teacher becomes coaching Jason through the hard work cycle, until he finally "tastes" success. After several of these cycles, reluctant learners eventually begin to internalize these good feelings and gain confidence in their ability to succeed, and ~ finally ~ begin to become what we call "self-motivated."

I worked in a high school that was predominantly minority, with 35% Anglo students and less than two percent Asian students. Yet, when you looked at the list of valedictorians and salutatorians, you would see a highly disproportionate number of Asian surnames. When I went in to talk with students, I would ask them, "Do you think Asian students are smarter than you?" They would look at me like I was nuts for even asking and quickly respond, "Well, yeah ~ duh!!" On the instances where an Asian student was in the classroom, I would always ask, "These kids think you're smarter than them ~ how'd that happen?" In the over 100 times I have asked an Asian student that question, I have only received ONE response.

Contrary to what many people assume, the response has never been "I work hard" (Quite frankly, that was my objective the first time I asked. I clearly intended to prove to the rest of my students that it was their laziness that was the problem). Likewise, I have never had an Asian student chime up and say, "I study." Instead, without exception, Asian students have spoken of the unrelenting parent or adult who refuses to accept less; the "irascible and sometimes terrifying Coach Fitz" in their life who demands that they rise to the occasion; someone who has pushed them through the hard work cycle, until they have seen and tasted success on the other end. For them, the synapse fires: hard work **works.** They eventually come to motivate themselves through this cycle.

> ## RESEARCH ANCHOR
>
> **A study by Makri-Botsari in 2001 found that "students who felt unconditionally accepted by their teachers were more likely to be interested in learning and to enjoy challenging academic tasks..."**
>
> **Makri-Botsari (in Kohn, 2005)**

What you and I know is that many students arrive at high school without having made a similar connection in their own brain. They have yet to experience the cycle that goes into *becoming* responsible, *learning* self-motivation. Coaches know that they must sometimes drag students ~ kicking and screaming ~ through this hard work cycle, in order to build intrinsic motivation.

> ## RESEARCH ANCHOR
>
> **"When the classroom culture focuses on rewards, 'gold stars,' grades, or class ranking, then pupils look for ways to obtain the best marks rather than to improve their learning."**
>
> **Black and Wiliam, 1998**

Within a coaching framework, grading practices must allow for students to be pushed through the hard work cycle and still receive the reward at the end, rather than having the bumps and detours during the cycle "averaged in" to an ending assessment that reflects the journey, and not the current performance. Coaching classrooms use problems and mistakes as opportunities for positive learning, not blame or baggage. Scores during scrimmages and practice are used as tools for improvement, and it is the *final score* that matters.

KEY POINT

Compliance or Competency

Academic consequences for behaviors stifle motivation to learn.

If you have been telling students ~ as an external motivator ~ that now that they are in high school it is time to start worrying about their GPA, you have been misinforming them. Ask any university admissions office why they tend to *discount* grade point averages, and they will give you three solid reasons:

1. There is a wide discrepancy between what an "A" or a "C" means between one high school and another.

2. There is a wide discrepancy between what an "A" or a "C" means between one teacher and another.

3. High school grades reflect behavior and compliance, as much as they do competency in the content area.

If you are sweet, come every day, bring supplies, and try hard, you are likely to pass, even though you may have less than satisfactory mastery of the course content. Likewise, if you are a difficult student, acting out, who rarely listens or turns in homework yet could ace a cumulative final your grade is likely to suffer.

If you give points for affective behaviors, such as bringing materials or being on time, you are not being fair to the student or the receiving institution, by giving them a higher grade than actually reflects their solid mastery of the content. Making an effort should not be enough to pass; the effort has to result in completed work of acceptable quality. Conversely, if you take away points for being a procrastinator or for not following the rules, and give a student a lower grade than actually reflects the solid mastery of the content, you are also doing a disservice.

GRADING PRACTICES

Marzano, 2000

Marzano conducted a review of grading practices in 2000. What was found is depicted in the table presented below.

Percentage of Teachers Reporting Use of Effort, Behavior, Cooperation, and Attendance in Determining Grades

Grade Levels	Effort	Behavior	Cooperation	Attendance
4-6	30%	8%	8%	10%
7-9	36%	10%	8%	18%
10-12	36%	14%	9%	24%

90/90/90 schools have also learned to send the message, "It's not where you start here that matters. It is your willingness to improve, to work hard, and to reach what you are capable of." Averaging is not in line with best practice. As Doug Reeves points out ~ giving a zero is not only bad educational practice, it is bad math. As a brief exercise, consider the information in the exercise provided below.

EXERCISE

As a brief exercise, consider the information provided below. Five students are characterized, with grades on three consecutive assignments. Two get "A's", two get "C's", and one gets a "D."

	Assessment Grades	Transposition to Letters	Averaging or Learning?
Student #1	55, 75, 95	75 average or "C"	?
Student #2	55, 75, 95	end point = "A"	?
Student #3	88, 95, 95	93 average or "A"	?
Student #4	75, 72, 78	75 average or "C"	?
Student #5	0, 95, 95	63 average or "D"	?

Is the *learning* the same or different for students #1 and #2? (same scores)

Is the *learning* the same of different for students #1 & #4? (same letter grade)

Is the *learning* the same or different for students #s 1, 2, 3, & 5? (same end)

Which grading practices reflect academic learning?

Which grading practices reflect averaging?

Our goal should be students who know, remember, and use what we teach them, not students who just do what we tell them.

RESEARCH ANCHOR

"The giving of marks and the grading function are overemphasized, while the giving of useful advice and the learning function are underemphasized."

Black and Wiliam, 1998

The power in the coaching framework is that the pre-game preparation normally reduces non-compliance in the first place. More students are willing to do the work, work hard, meet deadlines, and strive for quality because they have had a voice in the design, and know they are part of a team goal. However, the coaching framework is clearly built on competency, rather than compliance. Students come to know that it is about learning rather than grades, and about feeling good rather than being rewarded for "acting right."

Coaching Reluctant Learners **A Practical Framework for Classroom Success**

KEY POINT | ## The Myth of the Zero

Unproductive behaviors are best remedied with behavioral consequences ~ NOT academic ones!

RESEARCH ANCHOR

"The most important purpose for grades is to provide information or feedback to students and parents. Research unquestionably supports the importance of feedback to specific learning goals. To illustrate, after reviewing 7,827 studies on learning and instruction, researcher John Hattie (1992) reported that providing students with specific information about their standing in terms of particular objectives increased their achievement by 37 percentile points."

Marzano, 2000

If it is OUR job to get kids to learn, and part of our job may become the willingness to *drag them to success*, what is the rationale for a "zero?" Is our goal to punish them, or to teach them to be responsible?

The power in the coaching framework is that the pre-game preparation normally reduces non-compliance in the first place. More students are willing to do the work, work hard, meet deadlines, and strive for quality because they have had a voice in the design, and know they are part of a team goal. However, the coaching framework is clearly built on competency, rather than compliance. Students come to know that it is about learning rather than grades, and about feeling good rather than being rewarded for "acting right."

If it is to teach them to be responsible, then it is very easy to prove. Once you have given Jason a zero, he has changed his ways, seen the light of day. If ten points off a day for late work is in place, then as soon as a student has lost those points, they begin turning in things on time, forever after.

Now look in your grade book. If you have students with multiple zeroes, then you **cannot** say you have taught that child to become responsible. If you have students who habitually turn in work late, then ten points off is not working to motivate *them* to turn in work on time. So what does? If you are not getting the desired result, then you must explore other approaches to influencing behaviors.

Even though the coaching framework serves to get most students on-the-field and in-the-game, there are still those sitting on the bench, or hanging out in the locker room, neglecting or refusing to do their part. Students should know that they cannot "opt" out of doing work. If it is not enough to know that you are letting yourself and the team down, then there will be a consequence. Failure to turn in work is not an academic problem ~ it is a behavioral problem with academic consequences. Turning in work late is not an academic problem ~ it is a behavioral problem with academic consequences.

Coaching classrooms *begin* with empowering student voice, utilizing student choice, matching assignments and assessments to what matters most, and setting up positive supports for hard work, in order to create a climate where behaviors that increase learning are willingly embraced. Nonetheless, not every student will change unproductive patterns easily. Just remember, unproductive behaviors need to be remedied with behavioral, not academic consequences. One consequence could be that they MUST take their OWN TIME (best done *immediately,* and during a social opportunity ~ lunch, before school, after school) to fulfill their responsibilities. A much better deterrent, and a much quicker route to responsible behavior, is to apply this behavioral consequence, rather than the ill-fated "gift" of not making them do the work to the level you demand. A bad grade is merely a reprieve to a reluctant learner... a lesser expectation that accepts a lower level of performance.

In effect, the myth of the zero also explodes the myth of which teacher has "high expectations." The philosophy in a coaching framework is to be a high standards classroom where EVERY child is successful. Coaching teachers believe that the agreement they made when they were hired, was to hold their students and themselves to that bar. Giving zeroes does not mean you have higher standards, it signifies that your standards are lower. You are expecting less from the child, and less from yourself as the teacher. It is easier to get a zero, than to do the work. It is easier to give a zero, than take the time to make the student come in and do the work.

RESEARCH ANCHOR

"The real alternative to making children suffer for their offences [or profit from doing as told] is to work *with* them to solve problems. *A working with* approach asks more of the teacher than a *doing to* strategy, but it's a good deal more effective."

Kohn, 2005

By the way, this should be applied to failing work, as well as failure to turn in work. Traditional teachers will roll their eyes, and say you are lowering standards by letting students do it over. Coaching teachers know you are not *letting* them do it over; you are MAKING them do it over. Traditional teachers "talk" about higher standards. Coaching teachers will get teams to REACH higher standards.

Do not let folks say, "Oh, you don't get a chance to do things over in the real world." Hogwash! There are countless opportunities and **requirements** for doing things over, until you get it right, in the real world. Ask any author, any scientist, any carpenter, or any mechanic.

Traditional teachers frequently talk about the "unfairness" of providing "second chances" for students. In one way they are right: you can't have the consequence for some, and not others. You have to have a clear, consistent, and immediate system for making students perform this high. I actually had a teacher once ask, "But if I make the failing student come in and pass, then the student who made a B will want to come in and make an A. That would be a good thing, wouldn't it!?" What is fair to students, is to see that hard work works, that teachers care enough about them to make them succeed, that school is about learning content, and that the accomplishment feels good at the end. If students know they will be **made, on their own time, to perform to quality,** and that hard work works and feels good, they are much more likely to display initiative, and "learn" to be responsible.

Changing grading practices is definitely swimming against the cultural current. Attempts to make these changes are likely to get you called "soft" on academics. In *Failure is NOT an Option*, Alan Blankstein describes the need to confront behaviors that are part of this myth, such as the teacher who says, "This is the way I get them ready for college. I'm very tough on them. I teach responsibility. I'm not going to enable them like some other teachers do." (Blankstein, 2004) Do not allow traditional teachers the *excuse* of "enabling" through lower expectations. **Our job is to ENABLE students to LEARN.** The best way to learn is to do the work. Likewise, do not allow teachers the *excuse* of "we're preparing them for college." **The best way to prepare students for college is for them to learn the material, and they can't learn the material if they don't do it.** Should teachers determine to take the path of least resistance, and remain with traditional "zero" and "ten points off" policies... at least they need to acknowledge it is a less demanding path.

KEY POINT

Homework

The effective consequence of NOT doing the work, is DOING the work!

As blunt as this may sound, it realistically points out two problems with homework frequently identified in the research: homework must be meaningful to the student and to the course content. Authentic homework assignments, parsed for purpose and meaning, where students have had a voice in designing ~ or at least choosing from ~ challenging and meaningful options result in greater compliance and greater learning.

Larry Bell says that asking students to do a homework assignment and then giving them a zero when they don't turn it in can only mean one of two things:

1. It means that the assignment was not of significant import that failure to do it in any way impeded the ability of the student to come back into the flow of the classroom content. For example, they can "not" know what was in the homework and still perform acceptably during the class the next day.

2. Or... you simply don't care that *that* student doesn't know it.

If teachers lament about students who do not turn in homework and wonder what to do to get them to comply, there may be a much more significant problem, and more important questions that need to be asked:

- Do homework and assignments reflect the rigor and relevance that engage students in the learning?

- Do homework assignments reflect *quantity* or **quality**?

- Are there supports and teaching strategies in place that engage students in the learning, and motivate them to complete assignments?

- Are relationships in place that help to accomplish the above?

- Have students had a voice in identifying the role of homework assignments in meeting their team goal?

Teachers who have multiple zeroes in their grade books for incomplete homework assignments need some assistance in how to capture the brains and hearts of today's students, in ways that get them to perform on challenging work. We cannot continue to apply yesterday's teaching practices for students who will be living in tomorrow's world.

Richard Strong closes *Teaching What Matters Most* with the story of the sixth grade teacher who entered his mind, never to be forgotten; a teacher who began the first fifteen minutes of the first day of school talking about how growing up, he had only heard adults tell him how *he* should be responsible, and never heard them talk about what *they* were responsible for. So he wanted to make sure his classroom knew what they could count on, from him as a teacher:

- You can count on me to take your thoughts and questions seriously.

- You can count on me to show you clearly how to do the work I assign.

RESEARCH ANCHOR

Student achievement can improve as much as 28% if homework is done well. Homework effectiveness ranges from a 12% increase for grades 7-9, up to 24% increase in achievement outcomes for grades 10+.

If assigned, homework must be graded (+28%), and preferably commented on (+30%) or its potential for helping student achievement plummets to a fraction of the impact.

Marzano, Pickering and Pollock, 2001

- You can count on me to help you find out why what we study is important, and how it is connected to your life now and in the future.

- You can count on me never to belittle your mistakes and errors, but to show you how to overcome them and learn from them. (Strong, 2001)

- You can count on me to nag and nudge you to success until you can succeed on your own. (Strong, 2001)

This teacher understood that responsibility is meaningless if it's not mutual, and that mutual responsibility creates a climate where more students are willing to not only complete, but to work hard on challenging assignments.

The research from the Southern Regional Education Board's *High Schools That Work* division sites the need for an A, B, C, Not Yet system of grading. This does not mean that we succumb to grade inflation, where what used to be worth a D now becomes a C because we don't want to fail a student. It means, instead, that we intend to hold students to the performance standards required in the real world. Students are held accountable to EARN a passing grade through multiple reworking of assignments, until they reach the quality that is demanded.

Likewise, the research catalogued in *Effort and Excellence in Urban Classrooms* illustrates that expecting ~ and getting ~ success with all students is manifested by teachers who insist that students complete every assignment.

"In our minds, this action probably is most central to putting an 'It's my job' philosophy into motion and may be the most powerful mechanism by which this philosophy leads to closing the achievement gap. Put simply, if an assignment is worth doing, it is worth completing... Completing each assignment should be viewed as paving the way to success... On the other hand, allowing incomplete assignments or accepting assignments that have been completed poorly creates diversions on the path to high achievement." (Corbett, Wilson, and William, 2002)

Completing assignments achieves the connection that hard work works. One of the best examples of the *"It's my job"* philosophy took place in a 90/90/90 classroom on an afternoon in Los Fresnos, Texas. When I asked how this teacher had managed to get these demographically ~ and attitudinally-challenged students to all turn in homework, she said simply, "I just hunt 'em down like a dog." She went on to tell the story of Raul, a student who "tested my last nerve, but I finally got through to him." It seems that after once again refusing to turn in work, Gabriella stood waiting for Raul outside of his last period class, and walked him to her room. "I stood over him the entire time as he grudgingly completed the assignment. I alternately prodded and encouraged but I refused to give in until he had done every bit of it. Then I graded it right then, shook his hand and said, 'I'll be darned, you made a 72; now don't make me hunt you down like a dog next time.' As soon as he left, I got on the phone and called his mama and said, 'Just wanted you to know how proud I am of Raul for coming in after school to get his homework done.'"

RESEARCH ANCHOR

Watson suggests we send a message to resistant learners such as, "You know what? I really like you. You can keep doing all this stuff and it's not going to change my mind. It seems to me that you are trying to get me to dislike you, but it's not going to work. I'm not ever going to do that."

In Kohn, 2005

Gabriella not only understood what would "get through" to Raul, she also understood the concept of double jeopardy. The most effective consequence for not doing the work IS DOING THE WORK. She didn't have to also punish him again, by also giving him a lower grade than if he'd "just done it the first time." By coaching Raul through the hard work cycle and letting him taste success at the end, she sent him two important messages:

1. You are capable of passing and passing feels good
2. I care enough about you to make you pass.

That's how you TEACH responsibility. That represents not only a much higher standard, but a much quicker way to create students who become self-motivated. Gabriella can coach for me anytime!

For one example of engaging today's kids more successfully in homework, See page 155 in Chapter 6.

Coaching classrooms learn to have behavioral consequences for behaviors, and NOT ACADEMIC consequences for behaviors.

Coaching gets reluctant learners to complete the success cycle.

Chapter FOUR *Checklist for Success*

☐ Are assignments and assessments linked to power standards?

☐ Have students had a voice in identifying the role of homework assignments in meeting their team goal?

☐ Do I give less homework, but the homework assignments I do give reflect increased rigor and increased relevance?

☐ Are homework assignments talked about in pre-game preparation, as a means of practice to improve skills?

☐ Do students have the opportunity to design high-interest/high-level homework assignments that extend their learning in meaningful ways?

☐ Are students ever given choices on which assignments, the length of assignments, or when to complete assignments?

☐ Do my grading practices reflect content mastery, rather than incorporating behavior and compliance?

☐ Do my grading practices provide assessments for learning without "averaging in" those assessments to the final grade?

☐ Do I have a "back-up" plan for non-compliance that utilizes a behavioral consequence, rather than an academic consequence?

With all these pieces in place, you are ready to transform from teaching to coaching. All you need is *just enough* support.

Chapter **FIVE** *What Do I Need* **to Make This Work?**

OVERVIEW

During my teaching career, I've had the good fortune to attend some outstanding professional development conferences, packed with thought-provoking ideas and proven strategies. On the trip home, my mind would be racing with plans for implementation in my classroom.

Then that pesky Monday morning would roll around: six periods to teach, 170 teenagers, three separate preps, club meetings to sponsor after school, department meetings before school, and progress reports looming. I would once again tumble into the vortex: the chaotic life of a high school teacher and the incredible gravitational pull of *school as usual*.

Months later, while cleaning off my desk in search of a paper Jason swore he had turned in, I would come across the file from that conference. A wistful, *wishful* sigh escapes before I look up and say, "It's not here. Have you looked through your backpack?"

Our biggest fear is that even if you find this book useful and exciting, Monday morning will swoop over you. The ideas and determination you have now will get filed away in your head, or on your desk.

For that reason, Chapter Five is devoted to some last-ditch tips for support and sustainability. If you really want to take these words off the page and into the classroom, here's what you will need:

KEY POINT

Just Enough Nerve...

What is needed is the courage to take a risk ~ to reach learners that have grown immune to our best efforts.

What is required at the individual level to produce sustainable changes in thinking and practice **is thinking and practice.** As much as we have tried to reassure you that the coaching framework is based on solid research and proven best practices, it is *always* risky to try new things. Particularly when colleagues may look at you askance, skeptical of student "voice," or your ability to "slow down and pare down," yet still *increase* learning outcomes.

Perhaps you have a period or two during the day that is packed with Emilys who are eager and successful. Our advice? Keep on doing what you're doing! It's working just fine. But, perhaps there is a period during the day or a unit within a course, where you are willing to take the plunge. You have not been getting maximum mileage in previous efforts ~ your motor is racing, the wheels are rapidly turning, but the "traction" seems minimal. Yet, you are determined to try ~ at least ~ the three simple pieces in the coaching framework.

Grab the *Game Plan Brainstorming* sheet on the following page, then grab a friend, and a soda, and ~ together ~ come up with what these three pieces below might look like, specifically with your unit and your kids.

1. Prior to beginning the unit, you coach the students into looking ahead at the chapter or the materials. You "force" them to make some decisions about what pieces within the unit look more important than others. You continually press them to determine for themselves what might be useful, might be interesting, might be difficult. THEN, you surprise them by showing them the test ahead of time! Once again, they have to think about and talk about which questions matter most, and how to do well. NOW, simply reassure them you are all in this together, and set a team goal. You're off!

RESEARCH ANCHOR

"Knowledge of one's individual learning style, and learning how to use style preferences can produce great academic gain. Without explicit instruction in self-monitoring and performance analysis, the reflective learning system of the brain can go dreadfully underdeveloped.

We need to teach students reflective thinking and meta-cognition deliberately, in a consistent manner, until students internalize the process."

Given, 2002

2. During the middle of this unit, give some sort of "test" or assessment, and grade it. The conversation now becomes about which pieces went well and for whom, and which pieces need improvement. Students also get to talk about how YOU ~ the teacher ~ can do better, as well as their own changes. Let them give ideas for the second half to each other, and to you. Set a new goal or approach to the goal, together. Then let them know this was an assessment FOR learning, and it is *only* the final score that matters! You're off again.

3. At the end of the unit, take the "test." See how you **all** did, and take some personal coaching ownership in their successes and failures. Talk about it. What did they learn that mattered? In what ways did they learn that worked? Did this seem different? In what ways better? In what ways harder? Let them know that the first time you try any new design, there are implementation hurdles. Seek their advice on ways to improve the framework, improve your role as coach, and improve themselves. Then try it again.

Brainstorming Sheet for KEY GAME PLAN ELEMENTS

Unit Game Plan for (Topic/Course) _____

Coached by _____

Pre-Game Preparations

Step ONE   Scouting the Unit _____

_____

Scouting the Students _____

Power Standards _____

Step TWO   What Victory and Quality Look Like _____

Game/Coaching Plan _____

Step THREE   Psyching Up for the Game _____

_____

On-the-Field and In-the-Game

Step FOUR   Scrimmage and Practice _____

Step FIVE   The Half-Time Report _____

Step SIX   Second Half ~ Increasing Performance _____

_____

Post-Game Reflections

Step SEVEN   Post Game Celebrations _____

Step EIGHT   Next Game Films _____

_____

Donegan, Greenleaf, and Wells-Papanek, 2006

There is a trade-off in any new venture, where the learning curve makes participants uncomfortable, and stumbles occur before benefits accrue. Hang in there. The rewards will begin to accumulate. Less time at home at night planning lectures and assignments, as you coach students to become more competent at constructing and planning their own learning. Less time at home correcting papers, as assessments become fewer yet more rigorous, and worthy of being self-assessed and discussed during class-time. Increased student motivation, higher student achievement, and fewer attendance and discipline problems, as students begin to see themselves as useful members of a team where freedom, power, autonomy, FUN AND ACCOMPLISHMENT are part of the classroom design. You will never go back to school as usual.

KEY POINT

Just Enough Permission...

What administrators, parents and teachers really want to see... are results.

Frequently, teachers will tell us, "I'd love to try this, but our principal makes us document all the standards," or "our department makes us use a pacing guide," or "our district makes us give a common assessment." None of these exclude your ability to move from teacher to coach, to increase student voice and choice, or even to concentrate on power standards. Students who are taught to depth and complexity what matters most, will perform as well *or better* on common assessments, even if you never got to "some" of the questions on the test. You can keep intermittent pace with your colleagues, yet spend more time during the period on "must knows," allowing time for student voices to be heard, and choices to be made. And, during the pre-game activity, students can identify and record on the board, *for you,* the standards and benchmarks they have determined are worthy opponents. Teachers are sometimes most fearful of the move from the front of the classroom to a coaching framework, because they think that when administrators walk into the room they expect to see you in front of the class disseminating information. Remind yourself that what they *really* want to see is results. When more students begin to work harder on more challenging assignments and the achievement rates begin to rise, that is the most valid "permission slip" of all.

The most important permission you need is from yourself, and your students. Take the time, up front, to talk about how and when school seems to "work" and "make sense" to them, and how to create and utilize a coaching framework in the classroom. Give each other permission and support to risk, to try, to fail, to fix it, to retry, to win, and to ENJOY a new approach to learning.

Also give yourself permission to take small steps and let success accumulate gradually. Trying too much, too fast, can create a frustration that may dissuade you altogether. Keep current practices that are working well for you. Try one part of the framework at a time, and then, when it, too, is working well, you will feel comfortable taking the next step.

KEY POINT

Just Enough Information...

Accurate, useful feedback in "real-time" leads to continual improvement.

Many teachers have a gut feeling that school as usual, is not working for many of their students, and have been implementing parts of the coaching framework instinctively. Now, you have the ability to tie your application of what "feels right" to research.

The success of schools and classrooms that have implemented a student-centered constructivist and collaborative approach, with teacher as coach and students as teams, has warranted an increase in both literature and professional development surrounding these practices. Learning opportunities abound. We encourage you to continue building understanding by looking at models and practices related to your content area.

> "This model represents a seismic shift ~ from annual to short-term. Instead of trying to "reform" a school or system, we should be creating the conditions for teams of teachers to continuously achieve (and receive recognition for) short-term wins in specific instructional areas (e.g., where assessment data indicate that students are struggling). Our plans, our "systemic reform," should focus primarily on establishing and sustaining the structure for just such norms of continuous improvement. (Schmoker, 2004)

You can always refer back to Chapter Three as you gather ideas for pre-game, half-time, and post-game. As you gain confidence and comfort with the coaching framework, you can revisit it again as you expand into scrimmages, micro-feedback loops, practice and coaching sessions, and new ways of grading and assessing FOR increased learning. In addition, Chapter Six, "Resources ~ Read More About It," allows you to build a research and resource base on each of the previous chapters.

Our intention was to provide you with enough information in the *Research and Results* section of each chapter to validate your willingness to risk a new classroom approach. We also wanted to make sure you had ammunition at your disposal in discussions where you begin recruiting colleagues to field test with you. As you encounter the natural reticence to change within yourself or the resistance from others, a review of the achievement results will help you provide solutions to identified barriers, and answers to hard questions.

Sharing this information with the district office may encourage the use of staff development time to support skills related to a student-centered classroom. Sharing this information with your campus administration may encourage the adaptation of existing observations and evaluations, to reflect an emphasis on *learning* rather than teaching. And the sharing of this information with peers may encourage others to provide you with additional ideas and supports, for your own development of coaching skills and strategies.

Of course, the best and most important information will come from your students, at the end of each unit. It is their advice and insight that will best inform your own increased success. The continuous improvement cycle built within the coaching framework involves an ongoing evaluation, personal reflection, and modification of practices that ~ in effect ~ creates your own professional development.

KEY POINT

Just Enough Time...

One goal of the coaching framework is to save you time.

In the beginning, the coaching framework will require time and 'work,' as you make the necessary adjustments from teacher to coach. Then, it will require some refining as you test the framework on different units. It will take time to build comfort, and develop ownership in your own version of a coaching classroom: tailoring strategies, coaching, trying out, and revising. But after several practice runs, you will be amazed at how much time and work is 'saved,' and how many more students are 'motivated.' You will never go back to school as usual.

If you are reading this book over the summer, begin to think of dividing the classroom year up in the same way you distinguish the three elements embedded in any unit. If you begin with a coaching framework at the beginning of a new school year, you have the luxury of time to gather information and build team relationships. Spending time, up front, to create an atmosphere in the classroom where kids feel safe to take academic risks, where their ideas are not scoffed at, and where they can learn to take responsibility for their own learning will provide pay-offs all year long.

Our example in Chapter Three was a 15-day unit with two days used in pre-game preparation; one day used for formative assessments and midway meta-cognition; and one day used for reflection, revision, and celebration. This percentage of time would shift, depending on the length and materials allocated within any unit.

It is important to remember, however, that students are not used to taking this much responsibility, being this mentally active, "thinking about learning," or reworking to quality. In the beginning, their lack of skill and lack of comfort will make each piece of the coaching framework a slower process. The more time you spend, the more successfully they will master their roles in a coaching classroom. As they gain trust in you and confidence in themselves, and as they continue to practice each of the eight steps described in the coaching framework, their progress through those steps will become quicker for each subsequent unit.

The coaching framework does not require a great deal of time in preparing alternate lessons and alternate assessments, since most of the changes you make will be done *in* class, **with** students. However, it does require some pre-game peptalks to yourself, as you consider *alternate thinking* ~ how you will vary your approach into this unit, from "I do all the work for them and give all the materials to them," to "I coach them through the thinking/working struggle." And, it does require time to reflect and revise during half-time, and at the end of each unit.

Take advantage of time opportunities that already exist, to further discuss and reflect on this framework with colleagues: department meetings, in-service opportunities, or smaller collegial circles.

The single most important tip to remember about time is that *it takes more than one time to master the coaching framework*. Promise yourself you will try it with *at least* three units in a row, to give yourself enough time to build the momentum necessary to propel away from the same old gravitational orbit.

KEY POINT

Just Enough Friends...

Surround yourself with open minded and encouraging colleagues.

One way to sustain new attitudes and practices is by building a network of support. We encourage you to form inquiry groups and networks among your colleagues, to keep the vision alive.

Keep it simple. The first step is simply convincing a like-minded and fun colleague who teaches the same subject you do, to jump in the pool with you. Just like you're more likely to go to the gym with a friend, you are more likely to exercise coaching framework skills within a "buddy system." Set up a casual, collegial time when the two of you can tackle a unit together. Use the brainstorming sheet provided on page 123. The most logical arrangement for support would be to meet prior to pre-game, over half-time, and at the post-game reflection. Make sure one of the goals of these meetings is to support each other through trying it, for at least three units. (It takes a while at the gym before you really start getting in shape, and feeling the benefit of your conditioning.)

As success begins to build, these conversations will not only maintain momentum, but the collective creativity will provide additional, reflective insights, to speed your own forward progress. Plus, they will be a refreshing departure from some of the typical teacher-lounge talk surrounding reluctant learners!

In *Telling Stories of Change*, McCombs quotes a teacher saying:

> *"I'm probably more stimulated that I have ever been in my 15 year career... It seems we have so many exciting ideas to share that whenever we have a free minute, we want to spend that time together, figuring out what to do with these new ideas. I don't ever remember being that enthusiastic when I was using traditional curriculum and instruction. I remember lunches where we did a lot of complaining but that doesn't happen in our office anymore. So for me, I think that's been the most invigorating part."*

Ideally, your school would provide the time and opportunity for you to participate in a professional learning community or lesson study circle with a small group of colleagues, over the course of a semester or year. The book, *On Common Ground*, points out there is an astonishing level of agreement in the research, that the most effective strategy for sustaining substantive improvement is the simple concept of starting with a group of teachers who meet regularly to develop, "field test," and measure instructional improvement strategies. (Dufour, et. al. , 2005)

KEY POINT

Just Enough Data...

Keeping track from the beginning will give rise to more celebrations along the way.

As you become comfortable with changes in practice, as well as with ongoing assessment and evaluation of the effectiveness of these changes (evidenced by increased student motivation, learning, and achievement), looking at the data will serve to bolster positive attitude toward ongoing learning and change ~ in your and your students. When we can look at the success of our efforts in concrete ways with colleagues, we recapture the excitement and enthusiasm of knowing we are making a difference in the learning and lives of more students.

RESEARCH ANCHOR

"Educators who want to ensure student learning must make use of formative assessment and feedback. Formative assessments are standards-based but have as their sole purpose student learning; There are no immediate consequences for poor performance ~ thus no high stakes. These are designed only to support learning."

Danielson, 2003

Part of what you want to build into your coaching framework is the ongoing tracking of incremental improvement. When you talk with students during pre-game, consider designing ways to measure forward progress. These might include affective measurements such as attitude surveys or attendance records, as well as individual, team or class achievement charts.

Whether setting up measurements with colleagues or with the students themselves, remember to make them specific and short-term. The key to momentum is to achieve and celebrate a continuous succession of small, quick victories in vital areas. Help your students "win small, win early, and win often."

As a classroom, make plans to share the results with other classes, and with parents. As colleagues, make plans to share the results with other colleagues, and with administration. The best way to build "buy in," is to prove progress.

WINNING THE BATTLE

Goodbye for Now... and Good Luck!

What happened on October 25, 1415? Come on, now... military historians consider it to be one of the most famous battles in military history. October 25, 1415. Here's a hint: Shakespeare wrote an entire play around this date. October 25, 1415!

The Battle of Agincourt may actually live inside some subset of some benchmark of some state's social studies standards, but ~ of course ~ it is not the exact date that is the power standard worth remembering forever, but the *reasons* and the *stories* and the *moral lessons* that resulted from the battle itself and its retelling.

At the risk of offending Shakespeare aficionados, I will summarize the battle quickly. A young, inexperienced king had traveled to France with a rag-tag group of equally inexperienced volunteers. They were sick, without food, and downright scared as they looked at the fires and tents on the hill above, where a well-rested, well-fed, well-equipped army of French noblemen and mercenaries outnumbered the British over 8 to one. Henry V gathered his comrades around him in the dark, rainy, and mud-laden terrain and offered them the chance to go home that night. Then he added, "But if you decide to stay, we are enough ~ perhaps ~ to beat them. And since tomorrow is a holiday at home, IF we win, every St. Crispin's Day from this year on they will celebrate our victory. Perhaps we *are* just enough to win, '**we few, we happy few, we band of brothers.**'" At the end of the next day, almost 6,000 French troops lay dead, while the English lost less than 400.

Shakespeare would suggest that it was comradeship and resolve that won the battle. Military historians would suggest it was the first major use of the British longbow. I would suggest that both are correct.

IN SUMMARY

With the changes in society, economy, public policy, state budgets, and district mandates ~ there is no doubt that the odds are daunting. Yet, every day, we keep fighting for successes, persisting. It is our hope that this book has added a framework with some accompanying new and effective tools for your arsenal. Now, find those kindred spirits who are willing to face this challenge with you, use the *right* approach, tools and framework for today's kids... and *stick together*! Public high schools need you. Jason needs you. Emily needs you, too. **Victory lies ahead.**

Revisiting Metaphors
ASSESSMENTS FOR AND OF LEARNING OVER TIME

We understand that not all readers are sports enthusiasts. Still, the metaphor works quite well to illustrate the *teacher-as-coach* framework. Below is a table that illuminates parallels across multiple metaphors ~ in hopes that readers will understand that the football metaphor is transferable in many ways.

	ATHLETIC COACH	**SCHOOL TEACHER**	**MUSIC INSTRUCTOR**
ANNUAL	End of Season	End of Year Standardized Test	After Final Concert
MID-YEAR	Mid-Season	End of Course or Mid-year Exams	After the Fall or Winter Concert

All items below presume that assessments are generated and key learning targets are known *prior* to instruction.

	ATHLETIC COACH	**SCHOOL TEACHER**	**MUSIC INSTRUCTOR**
END OF SEGMENT	End of Game	End of Unit or Chapter	After a Musical Piece is Completed
MID-SEGMENT ~ MID-UNIT	Half-Time Adjustments before returning to the field:	Mid-Unit/Chapter as a formative assessment ~ linked to desired learning outcomes:	Section by Section in a new piece, stopping to make corrections along the way:

OBJECTIVES	▪ Game Film Reviews
	▪ Reading Defenses
	▪ Content Knowledge
	▪ Requisite Skills
	  ✓ blocking
	  ✓ body position
	  ✓ timing
	  ✓ anticipate play
	  ✓ running routes
		▪ Target Power Standards
		▪ Emphasize Learning Objectives, ie:
		  ✓ paragraph formation
		  ✓ word choice
		▪ Key Content Knowledge
		▪ Requisite Skills
		  ✓ vocabulary
		  ✓ main idea
		  ✓ details
			▪ Master a Piece
			  ✓ clarinets
			  ✓ trumpets, etc.
			▪ Content Knowledge
			▪ Requisite Skills
			  ✓ time signature
			  ✓ key signature
			  ✓ dynamics (loud/soft)
			  ✓ pacing
			  ✓ reading the score
			  ✓ marching

FEEDBACK FREQUENCY How often is feedback (micro-assessments) provided regarding objectives?

During Game ~ All Along the Way	During Game ~ All Along the Way	During Game ~ All Along the Way

Chapter **SIX** *Resources* ~ **Read More About It...**

Brain Science and Learning

All teaching must be done with memory, recall, and retention in mind. Teaching for short-term measures (chapter, end of course, or standardized tests) may provide gains in the present, however, distract energies required for processing toward long-term memory and recall.

"The biological limits to our potential are relatively minimal compared to the cultural and environmental limits. There are sound and weak techniques of learning and teaching, more than bright and dull minds. We can now consider our own philosophy of teaching, our own goals for what will happen for our students, the methods we use... to help our students learn, and the outcomes we typically achieve."

Christian Jernstedt, 2004

Recent brain research has provided much insight into what it takes for today's learners to acquire, retain, and use new knowledge. The bottom line is straight forward:

S/he who works, learns.

In order for our curriculum to become part of the ongoing repertoire of a student, THEY must do the work necessary for THEIR brain to process sufficiently to create new connections. If a synapse is to "fire" and result in learning (a lasting memory), then it is only in the learner's brain that this can take place. Any attempt to short cut the requirement for processing simply will not produce long-term memory. Whenever possible, students must engage their own experiences, understandings, and thought processing if they are to create "networks" of connected, accessible knowledge.

Greenleaf, "*Brain Based Teaching*," 2005

NATURUAL LEARNING SYSTEMS

Recently, Dr. Barbara Given compiled an impressive array of timely, pertinent, and valid research. From this, she developed a viable, practical model for considering the brain's natural processing functions as they relate to the teaching/learning intersection. These five natural systems are cognitive, emotional, social, physical, and reflective.

Comprehensive systems for receiving, processing and recalling information are thoroughly integrated throughout brain areas. Though we see evidence of localized activity through fMRI and PET scan studies, these "areas of activity" do not represent ALL activity ~ they represent where the initial or most of the activity takes place. Still, it is important to understand that within moments other areas are involved in major, minor or peripheral ways. Bottom line: the brain is so integrated that localization of regional activity is useful for research purposes, but less directly applicable for instructional practice.

If we understand this model, then we are compelled to offer opportunities to learners that serve to prompt each learning system over the course of a unit of study or series of lessons. By doing so, we differentiate instructional approaches, vary strategies, prompt processing in working memory and build multiple pathways for retention, recall, transfer, and application of learnings... in short, for understanding. The five learning systems of the brain follow.

THE COGNITIVE LEARNING SYSTEM can be overrun by the stress response system and other perceived priorities.

- Interprets, stores, and retrieves information via patterns and pictures.
- Establishes integrated circuits of knowledge and skill.
- Actions that we perform based on an explicit intention.
- Requires integrated prior knowledge and skills.
- Enables us to read, write, and calculate.
- Enables us to interpret, store, and retrieve information.
- Can be overrun by stress response system and other perceived priorities.

THE EMOTIONAL LEARNING SYSTEM operates internal stress response activities and generates powerful vehicles for enhancing memory ~ or likewise powerful inhibitors and blockers.

- With personal meaning comes relevance and a passion for learning.

- Manages a learner's motivation, demeanor, and creativity.

- Emotions can empower and energize (or depress and stifle) all other learning systems.

- Class climate and emotional safety are closely linked to a student's success.

- Emotion is a powerful vehicle to enhance memory, manage our demeanor, and increase creativity.

THE SOCIAL LEARNING SYSTEM relates to our interactions with others ~ context of people.

- Articulation (speaking) generates additional memory paths.

- Social skills govern our interactions, collaboration, and communications with others.

- Through group membership, teamwork, and team accomplishments we acquire skills.

- By learning how to respect the productivity and attention of others, our interactions and interpersonal skills will improve.

- When students are considered a community of learners, they learn to build on the strength of working in pairs to problem-solve, to help integrate all five of the learning systems.

THE PHYSICAL LEARNING SYSTEM takes longer to establish, however it can lead to better sustained ~ procedural ~ comprehensive.

- Responsible for distributing information and prompting action throughout the brain, and body.

- Gathers information through all senses to direct us and where our body is in space.

- Physical encoding and engagement promotes connection and ownership.

- Learning is enhanced by being actively involved and by hands-on work.

- Movement and active practicing encourages the brain to work better.

THE REFLECTIVE LEARNING SYSTEM focus on "LEARNING" always operates within a context/setting ~ an environment that exists either physically or perceptually in the mind.

- Weighs past, present, and future projections.

- When we understand what to do under a given set of circumstances, our understanding, and knowing ourselves is increased.

- We interpret verbal and nonverbal cues via meta-cognition to monitor situations and to make decisions about our performance.

- Meta-cognates ~ in consideration through self-monitoring, and the analysis of one's own learning process and acquired knowledge... we understand our own learning style.

Given, "*Teaching to the Brain's Five Natural Learning Systems*," 2002

CLASSROOM INSTRUCTION THAT WORKS

INSTRUCTIONAL STRATEGIES

Marzano, Pickering, and Pollock conducted a review of educational research over the past 35 years, condensing that research into the salient practices that have the most impact on student achievement outcomes.

CATEGORY	PERCENTILE GAIN	CATEGORY	PERCENTILE GAIN
Identifying Similarities and Differences	45%	Cooperative Learning	27%
Summarizing and Note Taking	34%	Setting Objectives and Providing Feedback	23%
Reinforcing Effort and Providing Recognition	29%	Generating and Testing Hypotheses	23%
Homework and Practice	28%	Questions, Cues, and Advance Organizers	22%
Nonlinguistic Representation	27%		

Marzano, Pickering, Pollock ~ ASCD 2001

Categories of Instructional Strategies That Affect Student Achievement ~ Figure 1.3, p. 7

REFERENCES

Brain Sciences and Learning

Given, Barbara. "Teaching to the Brain's Natural Learning Systems," ASCD 2002.

Gordon, Barry. "Memory: Remembering and Forgetting in Everyday Life," New York: Mastermedia Ltd/Dana Alliance for Brain Initiatives; 1995.

Gordon, Barry and Berger L. Intelligent Memory. New York: Viking Press; Fall, 2003.

Greenleaf, Robert K. "Brain Based Teaching: Making Connections for Long-term Memory and Recall," Greenleaf & Papanek Publications, www.greenleaflearning.com, 2005.

Greenleaf, Robert K. & Wells-Papanek, Doris. "Memory, Recall, the Brain & Learning," (Former Title: "Knowledge Representation and the Brain,") Greenleaf & Papanek Publications, www.greenleaflearning.com, 2005.

Jernstedt, Christian. From Workshop Handouts/notes, Dartmouth College. 2005.

Schenck, Jeb. "Learning, Teaching and the Brain." Knowa@wyodino.org.

Professional Learning Communities *&*
Continuous Opportunities for Improvement

In fact, the most productive thinking is continuous and simultaneous with action ~ that is, when teachers ~ as practitioners ~ collaboratively implement, assess and adjust instruction as it happens.

Schmoker, 2003

"The consistent message of 90/90/90 schools is that the penalty for poor performance is not a low grade, followed by a forced march to the next unit. Rather, student performance that is less than proficient is followed by multiple opportunities to improve performance." "Most of the schools conducted weekly assessments of student progress. These assessments were not district or state tests, but were assessments constructed and administered by classroom teachers. The consequence of students performing badly was not an admonishment to 'Wait until next year' but rather the promise that 'You can do better next week.'"

"In fact, when students know that there are not additional opportunities to succeed, they frequently take teacher feedback on their performance and stuff it into desks, back packs, and wastebaskets. Students in this scenario are happy with a 'D' and unmotivated by an 'F'."

"In a classroom assessment scenario in which there are multiple opportunities to improve, however, the consequence for poor performance is not a bad grade and discouragement, but more work, improved performance, and respect for teacher feedback."

Reeves, 2003

"[for learning purposes]... a test at the end of a unit or teaching module is pointless; it s too late to work with the results. We concluded that the feedback on tests, seatwork, and homework should give each pupil guidance on how to improve, and each pupil must be given help and an opportunity to work on the improvement."

Black and Wiliam, 1998

The reflective learning system of the brain (one of five) serves to incorporate activities of the day/week with past activities. It is an important function of long-term memory, as it relies on prior experience and knowledge as it integrates new learning. Without this system, the other four systems [of the brain] can produce only limited results. This refers to the personal consideration of one's own learning... achievements, failures, what worked, what didn't and what needs improvement. This system weighs past, present, and probable thoughts and behaviors, then predicts future outcomes by asking self-directed questions.

Given, 2002

REFERENCES **Professional Learning Communities & Continuous Opportunities for Improvement**

Black, Paul & Wiliam, Dylan. "Assessment and Classroom Learning," Assessment in Education, March 1998, p. 7-74.

DuFour, Richard & DuFour, Rebecca. "On Common Ground: The Power of Professional Learning Communities," National Education Service, 2005.

DuFour, Richard & DuFour, Rebecca, Eaker, Robert & Karhanek, Gayle. "Whatever It Takes: How Professional Learning Communities Respond When Kids Don't Learn," National Education Service, 2004.

EdTrust, Kati Haycock, www.edtrust.org.

Fullan, Michael & Hargreaves, Andy. "What's Worth Fighting for in Your School?" Teachers College Press, 1996.

Given, Barbara. "Teaching to the Brain's Natural Learning Systems," ASCD 2002.

Schmoker, Mike. "Tipping Point: From Feckless Reform to Substantive Instructional Improvement," Phi Delta Kappan, February 2004.

Reeves, Douglas, B. "High Performance in High Poverty Schools: 90/90/90 and Beyond," www.makingstandardswork.com.

Stiggins, Rick. "Assessment Crisis: The Absence of Assessment FOR Learning," Phi Delta Kappan, June 2002, V 83, No. 10, p. 758-765.

Supovitz, Jonathan and Christman, Jolley Bruce, "Small Learning Communities That Actually Learn: Lessons for School Leaders," Phi Delta Kappan, May 2005.

Expectations

"...study concluded that students' intellectual development is largely a response to what teachers expect and how those expectations are communicated."

Rosenthal & Jacobson, 1987 (In Cotton)

The beliefs teachers themselves have about teaching and learning and the nature of the expectations they hold for students also exert a powerful influence (Raffini). As Deborah Stipek (1988) notes, "To a very large degree, students expect to learn if their teachers expect them to learn."

Stipeck, 1988

The most important finding from this research is that teacher expectations can and do affect students' achievement and attitudes. Among the research materials supporting this paper, all that address this topic found relationships between expectations and student outcomes.

How are high expectations for students communicated among staff members, to students, and to parents? Researchers cite the following:

- **Setting goals which are expressed as minimally acceptable levels of achievement** rather than using prior achievement data to establish ceiling levels beyond which students would not be expected to progress (Good, 1987)

- **Developing and applying policies which protect instructional time,** e.g., policies regarding attendance, tardiness, interruptions during basic skills instructional periods, etc. (Murphy, et al., 1982)

- **Establishing policies which emphasize the importance of academic achievement to students,** e.g., minimally acceptable levels of achievement to qualify for participation in extracurricular activities, regular notification to parents when academic expectations aren't being met, etc. (Murphy and Hallinger, 1985)

- **Having staff members who hold high expectations for themselves** as leaders and teachers, taking responsibility for student performance (Brookover and Lezotte 1979; Edmonds 1979; Murphy and Hallinger, 1985; Murphy, et al., 1982)

- **"Insistent Coaching"** of students who are experiencing learning difficulty (Good 1987; Taylor, 1986-87)

In Cotton, 2001

Major findings in the research on school-wide and teacher expectations include:

- Expectations, as communicated school-wide and in classrooms, can and do affect student achievement and attitudes;

- Teacher expectations and accompanying behaviors have a very real ~ although limited ~ effect on student performance, accounting for five to ten percent of student achievement outcome;

- Communicating *low expectations* has more power to limit student achievement than communicating high expectations has to raise student performance;

- A minority of teachers treat low-expectation students in ways likely to inhibit their growth, e.g., by exposing them to less learning material and material that is less interesting, giving them less time to respond to questions, and communicating less warmth and affection to them;

- When teachers engage in differential treatment of high- and low-expectation students, students are aware of these differences;

- Low-expectation students have better attitudes in classrooms where differential treatment is low than in classrooms where it is high;

- In the hands of some teachers, low groups and low tracks are subject to the same kinds of limiting treatment as are individual low-expectation students ~ with the same negative effects;

- The negative effects of differential teacher treatment on low-expectation students may be direct (less exposure to learning material) or indirect (treating students in ways that erode their learning motivation and sense of self-efficacy).

Given these findings, what can be done to improve the ways teachers form expectations and communicate them, especially to students they perceive as having limited potential? Recommendations are drawn from several authors:

- **Set goals** (for individuals, groups, classrooms, and whole schools) in terms of floors (minimally acceptable standards), not ceilings; communicate to students that they have the ability to meet those standards;

- **Use heterogeneous grouping** and cooperative learning activities whenever possible; these approaches capitalize on students' strengths and take the focus off weaknesses;

- **Develop task structures** in which students work on different tasks, on tasks that can be pursued in different ways, and on tasks that have no particular right answer to minimize harmful comparisons;

- **Emphasize that different students** are good at different things and let students see that this is true by having them observe one another's products, performances, etc.

- **Monitor student progress closely,** keeping expectations of individuals current.

- In giving students feedback, **stress continuous progress** relative to previous levels of mastery, rather than comparisons with statistical norms or other individuals;

- In giving students feedback, **focus on giving useful information,** not just evaluation of success or failure;

- **When students do not understand** an explanation or demonstration, diagnose the learning difficulty and follow through by breaking down the task or re-teaching it in a different way;

- **Think in terms of stretching the students' minds** by stimulating them and encouraging them to achieve as much as they can, not in terms of "protecting" them from failure or embarrassment.

Cotton, 2001

"It is also generally the case that only a few pupils in a class answer the teacher's questions. The rest then leave it to these few, knowing that they cannot respond as quickly and being unwilling to risk making mistakes in public. So the teacher, by lowering the level of questions and accepting answers from a few, can keep the lesson going but is actually out of touch with the understanding of most of the class."

Black and Wiliam, 1998

"Advocates of TESA say the real benefits come when teachers take an honest look at themselves as ask questions such as:

- How am I communicating my expectations to my students?

- Are my expectations different for my "high," "average," and "low" achievers? "

Center for Adolescent and Family Studies

REFERENCES **Expectations**

Black, Paul & Wiliam, Dylan. "Assessment and Classroom Learning," Assessment in Education, March 1998, p. 7-74.

Center for Adolescent and Family Studies ~ http://www.indiana.edu/~cafs/

Cotton, Kathleen. "Expectorations and Student Outcomes," 2001. http://www.nwrel.org/scpd/sirs/4/cu7.html.

Darling-Hammond, Linda. "Teacher quality and student achievement: a review of state policy evidence," cw.mariancollege.edu, 1999.

Rist, R.C. "Student Social Class and Teacher Expectations: The Self-Fulfilling Prophecy in Ghetto Education," EJ025119.

Stipek, Deborah. "Motivation to Learn: From Theory to Practice," Englewood Cliffs, New Jersey: Prentice Hall, 1988.

Feedback

Feedback is providing students with timely information relative to how well they are doing on *identified learning goals & objectives* throughout the unit of instruction.

- Explain what is accurate and what is inaccurate at intermittent and/or crucial/transitional times;

- Feedback must be timely ~ immediate or day after;

- Feedback needs to be specific to a criteria, informing students where they stand relative to a specific knowledge or skill component;

- Feedback can be provided by students themselves and/or by classmates;

- Timely feedback is required if adjustments to learning are to take place;

- Telling "right" or "wrong" has negligible effect if done after each item.

Some studies produced the following percentile gains when appropriate feedback was provided:

	Percent Increase
Lysakowski & Walberg, 1982	26%
Walberg, 1999	33%
Tennebaum & Goldring, 1989	25%
Kumar, 1991	41%
Sheerens & Bosker, 1997	36%

Adapted from Marzano, Pickering & Pollock, 2001

"… schools with significant improvements provided significantly more frequent feedback to students… in real time."

" teachers with large gains [in student achievement] were committed to feedback that was consistently accurate, with student performance compared to unambiguous expectations."

The "… best practice/s in assessment [are those] in which students are required to complete a task and then very soon ~ within minutes, hours or days ~ they receive feedback that is designed to improve their performance. Effective assessment is what great music educators and coaches routinely provide to their students."

Reeves 2003

"Feedback must be timely and unambiguous. It must be diagnostic in nature... it is necessary to establish learning goals and improve achievement outcomes. Administrators that encourage teachers to collect, organize, and evaluate school and classroom data to inform their practice can help improve a school."

Danielson, 2003

"While formative assessment [intermittent feedback] can help all pupils, it yields particularly good results with low achievers by concentrating on specific problems with their work and giving them a clear understanding of what is wrong and how to put it right."

Black and Wiliam, 1998

MICRO-FEEDBACK LOOPS ~ Provide very targeted data to teachers and students about one or two very specific learning needs within minutes or a day. The tenets for successful implementation are based on Interest, Usefulness, Doablility, a Discrete Focus, Collaboration on Student Work, and Regular (daily) Feedback. If the questions below can be answered with a "yes," then circumstances have been designed for success.

Regarding the Feedback Data Process

- Can you develop assessments in five minutes or less? (Doable/Feedback)

- Can you embed assessments in existing units/practice? (Useful/Focus/Interest)

- Can you score/enter data/gain feedback in five minutes (per class) or less? (Doable)

- Can the data be represented in a simple, easy to decipher manner? (Useful/Interest/Feedback)

Regarding Instructional Focus

- Can you adjust a facet of the existing lessons/unit to accommodate this shift? (Interest/Doable)

- Does each teacher believe the focus is important and worthy of their adjusted effort? (Interest/Useful)

Regarding Collaboration

- Do pairs/teams/departments (configurations) have designated or accessible time to share feedback and discuss student learning needs/work at frequent, determined intervals? (Doable/Collaborate/Feedback)

Process Developed by Greenleaf Learning, 2004

REFERENCES   Feedback

Black, Paul & Wiliam, Dylan. "Inside the Black Box: Raising Standards Through Classroom Assessment," Phi Delta Kappan, October 1998.

Chappius, Jan. "Helping Students Understand Assessment," Educational Leadership, November 2005, V 63 no.3, p. 39.

Costa, Arthur & Kallick, Bena. "Discovering & Exploring Habits of Mind," ASCD, 2000.

Cushman, Kathleen. "Fires in the Bathroom," What Kids Can Do, 2003.

Danielson, Charlotte. "Enhancing Student Achievement," ASCD, 2002.

Greenleaf Learning, Micro-Feedback Loops. www.greenleaflearning.com, 2004.

Marzano, Pickering & Pollock. "Classroom Instruction that Works," ASCD, 2001.

Reeves, Douglas, B. "High Performance in High Poverty Schools: 90/90/90 and Beyond," www.makingstandardswork.com.

Stiggins, Rick. "Assessment, Student Confidence, and School Success," Phi Delta Kappan, www.pdkintl.org/kappan/k9911sti.htm, August 2002.

Formative Assessments

Mid-course corrections provide opportunities for learning that precede final performance outcomes. Assessing *FOR* learning involves more than testing more frequently.

"These [90/90/90] schools consistently elevate the importance of classroom-based, teacher-made tests that are collaboratively scored and used to provide immediate feedback to both students and teachers."

"Moreover, great educators use assessment data to make real-time decisions and restructure their teaching accordingly."

Reeves, 2003

Implications for Assessment Practices

#1   Assessments must be a source of information for both students and teachers (no surprises embedded);

#2   Assessments need to be followed by high quality corrective instruction;

#3   Students must be given a second chance to show improvement.

Guskey, North Central Association, 2004

Three Stages to the Process of Assessing Learners

First   Determine student-learning goals;

Second   Collect, analyze and interpret evidence from multiple sources of data to determine how students are doing;

Third   Consider the root causes of present achievement levels and then ~ and only then ~ implement systematic actions to address root causes, promote enduring learning, and increase test scores.

Jay McTighe and Ronald S. Thomas, 2003

"Thus self-assessment by pupils, far from being a luxury, is in fact *an essential component of formative assessment*. When anyone is trying to learn, feedback about the effort has three elements: redefinition of the *desired goal*, evidence about *present position*, and some understanding of a *way to close the gap between the two*. All three must be understood to some degree by anyone before he or she can take action to improve learning."

"Upon pooling the information on the estimated effects of improved formative assessment ... they reported unprecedented positive effects on student achievement. ...improved formative assessment helps low achievers more than other students and so reduces the range of achievement [gap] while raising achievement overall."

Black and Wiliam, 1998

"[standardized tests] can reflect large-group increases or decreases in learning on an annual basis... [however] they cannot inform the moment-to-moment, day-to-day, week-to-week instructional decisions faced by students and teachers seeking to manage the learning process as it unfolds. They cannot diagnose student needs during learning, tell students what study tactics are/are not working, or keep parents informed about how to support their work of their children."

Stiggins, 2005

"When they assess FOR learning, teachers use the classroom assessment process and the continuous flow of information about student achievement that it provides in order to advance, not merely check on, student learning. They do this by;

- understanding and articulating *in advance of teaching* the achievement targets that their students are to hit;

- informing their students about those learning goals, *in terms that students understand*, from the very beginning of the teaching and learning process;

- using classroom assessments to *build students' confidence* in themselves as learners and help them take responsibility for their own learning, so as to lay a foundation for lifelong learning;

- translating classroom assessment results into frequent *descriptive feedback* (versus judgmental feedback) for students, providing them with specific insights as to how to improve;

- Continuously adju*sting instruction* based on the results of classroom assessments;

- Engaging students in *regular self-assessment*, with standards held constant so that students can watch themselves grow over time and thus feel in charge of their own success; and

- Actively involving students in co*mmunicating* with their teacher and their families about their achievement status and improvement."

Stiggins, 2002

REFERENCES **Assessment, Testing, and Data**

Assessment Reform Group. "Assessment for Learning: 10 Research-based Principles to Guide Classroom Practice," 2002.

Black, Paul & Wiliam, Dylan. "Inside the Black Box: Raising Standards Through Classroom Assessment," Phi Delta Kappan, October 1998.

Black, Paul & Wiliam, Dylan. "Assessment and Classroom Learning," Assessment in Education, March 1998, p. 7-74.

Guskey, Thomas. Presentation at the North Central Association annual meeting, 2003.

Marzano, Pickering, McTighe, "Assessing Student Outcomes," ASCD, 1993.

McTighe, Jay & Thomas, Ronald S. "Backward Design of Assessments," 2003.

Popham, W. James "The Truth About Testing: An Educator's Call to Action," ASCD, 2001.

Popham, W. James. "Assessment for Learning: An Endangered Species?" Educational Leadership, ASCD. February 2006.

Reeves, Douglas. Center for Performance Assessment on 90/90/90 Schools.

Schmoker, Mike. "Results, The Key to Continuous School Improvement," ASCD 1996.

Shepard, Lorrie A. "Linking Formative Assessment to Scaffolding." Educational Leadership, November 2005, V 63 no.3, p. 66.

Stiggins, Rick. "Assessment Crisis: The Absence of Assessment FOR Learning," Phi Delta Kappan, June 2002, V 83, No. 10, p. 758-765.

Stiggins, Rick. "Assessment, Student Confidence, and School Success," Phi Delta Kappan, www.pdkintl.org/kappan/k9911sti.htm, August 2002..

Stiggins, Rick and Chappius, Jan. "What a Difference a Word Makes," Journal of Staff Development, Winter 2006.

Stix, Andi. "The Art of Negotiable Contracting for Assessment," AGATE, Fall 2000.

White, Stephen H. "Beyond the Numbers: Making Data Work for Teachers & School Leaders," Advanced Learning Press, 2005.

Goal Setting *&* Power Standards

Goal setting is the process of establishing a direction for learning that identifies both short and long-term objectives. Setting Goals has been shown to have a potential, overall impact of +23% increase in academic achievement compared to when goal setting is not used.

Goal Setting Considerations

1. Narrow the focus of study (however, assure the instruction and assessment are aligned with the overall goals)

2. Maintain a general scope that accommodates the constructivist nature of learning differences (behavioral objectives have less impact, as they are too specific)

3. Student performance increases when they have the opportunity to personalize the "teacher's" overall goals for a unit of study.

Research Studies on Goal Setting as related to Student Performance

STUDY	PERCENT GAIN
Wise & Okey, 1983	41%
Walberg, 1999	18%
Lipsey & Wilson, 1993	21%

Adapted from Marzano, Pickering & Pollock, 2001

On Targeted Outcomes "[In the 90/90/90 schools it was common for]... every school to identify five areas in which they measured improvement. Although the school could choose the goal from a menu, the common requirement was to focus on a few indicators of improvement in contrast to the typical school improvement plan that contains a large number of unfocused efforts to improve. The focus on improvement is especially important in an environment where many students come to school with academic skills that are substantially below grade level."

Reeves, 2003

"Because we gather so much data... [that] reveal so many opportunities for improvement, we set too many goals and launch too many initiatives, over-taxing our teachers and our systems. Educators must *Focus, Focus, Focus.*

- Which data, well analyzed, can help us improve teaching and learning?
- Within an identified subject/course, where do we need to direct our attention?
- Where do the greatest number of students struggle or fail within the larger domains?

Schmoker, 2003

NINE Characteristics of Schools with Great Academic Gains
as Adapted from Reeves Work

1. **Collaboration**
   - Examination of student work
   - Collective determination of what "proficiency" means regarding student work; **NOT** idle discussion, simple friendly, collegial gatherings

2. **Feedback**
   - Much more feedback to students
   - Feedback provided in "real time"
   - Accuracy of feedback emphasized; **NOT** ambiguous, delayed, distorted

3. **Time**
   - Changes in schedule to accommodate priorities
   - More time give to "literacy" and "numeracy"; **NOT** moving players on the "chess-board"

4. **Action Research/Midcourse Correction**
   - Dynamic, ongoing, evolving process
   - Exploring & sharing ideas and options; **NOT** static, stale, past-history documents

5. **Aligning Teacher Assignments with Teacher Prep**
   - Decisive moves to align staff with interest, competence, & background training
   - Moving educators to different grades/subjects; **NOT** newest teachers get toughest class assignments

6. **Constructive Data Analysis**
   - Focus on student data from multiple sources
   - Cohort data vs. year to year (track same students); **NOT** comparing students to other students

7. **Common Assessments**
   - Teacher constructed
   - Student completes a task ~ receives feedback designed to improve performance; **NOT** more testing, but ~ more *assessing*

8. **Valuing Every Adult as a Resource for Students**
   - Inclusive professional development
   - All are part of the journey & impact students; **NOT** certified staff only, on isolated efforts

9. **Cross-Disciplinary Integration**
   - All subject areas are involved for transfer
   - Sub-sets of standards cut across areas, and as such, staff collaborate to address similar concepts; **NOT** a mere focus on tested subjects only.

REFERENCES **Goal Setting & Power Standards**

Ainsworth, Larry. "Unwrapping the Standards," Center for Performance Assessment, 2003.

Guskey, Thomas. "Mapping the Road to Proficiency," Educational Leadership, November 2005, V 63 no.3, p. 32.

Leahy, Siobhan; Lyon, Christine; Thompson, Marnie; & Wiliam, Dylan. "Classroom Assessment: Minute by Minute, Day by Day," Educational Leadership, November 2005

Marzano, Pickering & Pollock. "Classroom Instruction that Works," ASCD 2001.

Reeves, Douglas B. "Making Standards Work," Advance Learning Press, 2003.

Reeves, Douglas, B. "High Performance in High Poverty Schools: 90/90/90 and Beyond," www.makingstandardswork.com 2003..

Schmoker, Mike. "Up and Away," Journal of Staff Development, National Staff Development Council, Spring 2002.

Stiggins, Rick. "Assessment Crisis: The Absence of Assessment FOR Learning," Phi Delta Kappan, June 2002, V 83, No. 10, p. 758-765.

Strong, Richard W. et al. "Teachers What Matters Most: Standards and Strategies for Raising Student Achievement," ASCD 2001.

White, Michael. "Why We Hate Standards," July 2004 Newsletter, Center for Performance Assessment.

Grading

"Marking is usually conscientious but often fails to offer guidance on how work can be improved. In a significant minority of cases, marking reinforces underachievement and under-expectation by being too generous or unfocused. Information about pupil performance received by the teacher is insufficiently used to inform subsequent work."

"The giving of marks and the grading function are overemphasized, while the giving of useful advice and the learning function are underemphasized."

"When the classroom culture focuses on rewards, 'gold stars,' grades, or class ranking, then pupils look for ways to obtain the best marks rather than to improve their learning."

Black and Wiliam,1998

"The most important purpose for grades is to provide information or feedback to students and parents. The best referencing system for grading is content-specific goals: a criterion-referenced approach. Research unquestionably supports the importance of feedback to specific learning goals. To illustrate, after reviewing 7,827 studies on learning and instruction, researcher John Hattie (1992) reported that providing students with specific information about their standing in terms of particular objectives increased their achievement by 37 percentile points."

Marzano, 2000

Feedback must be timely and unambiguous. It must be diagnostic in nature... it is necessary to establish learning goals and improve achievement outcomes. Administrators that encourage teachers to collect, organize, and evaluate school and classroom data to inform their practice can help improve a school. "Educators who want to ensure student learning must make use of formative assessment and feedback. Formative assessments are standards-based but have as their sole purpose student learning; There are no immediate consequences for poor performance ~ thus no high stakes. These are designed only to support learning."

Danielson, 2002-03

REFERENCES

Grading

Bell, Larry. Multicultural America, Inc. www.larry-bell.com.

Black, Paul & Wiliam, Dylan. "Inside the Black Box: Raising Standards Through Classroom Assessment," Phi Delta Kappan, October 1998.

Canady, Robert. IDEA Institute Cassette and Video; 259 Regency Ridge, Dayton, OH 45459, 1994.

Danielson, Charlotte. "Enhancing Student Achievement," ASCD, 2002.

Marzano, Robert J. "Transforming Classroom Grading," ASCD 2000.

Marzano, Pickering, McTighe, "Assessing Student Outcomes," ASCD, 1993.

Homework

Homework Defined	Homework extends learning opportunities beyond the official school day times
Homework Goal	To provide high-quality, specific feedback, soon
Research	+/- 28% impact on student performance outcomes

USE OF HOMEWORK	PERCENTILE GAIN
Homework assigned, but not graded or commented on	11%
Homework graded, but without comments	28%
Homework graded, with teacher comments as feedback	30%

Adapted from Marzano et al. 2001

- The amount assigned should vary (increase) with age. Homework is more effective for older students:

grades 4-6	5%
grades 7-9	12%
grades 10-12	24%

- Parent involvement with homework should be kept to a minimum

- The purpose of homework must be clearly articulated

  Practice high degree of student familiarity, providing focused practice on a skill/knowledge set

  Elaboration as preparation for new concept or to extend already introduced content. Understanding principles underpinning knowledge is essential

- Homework environment: consistent, organized place; consistent schedule/time; sufficient prompts/encouragement; cease at a specific time, whether done or not

- Varied approaches to homework enhances motivation/interest

- Students may share in the tracking or scoring of some homework.

Homework Strategy

CLASSROOM STRATEGY ON HOMEWORK

Please realize that it will be harder to do this late in the year after habits and attitudes have formed. It is a great strategy to use at the beginning of a new school year.

Take a period prior to the next chapter/unit and say, "Hey guys, you know I think the only thing keeping us from getting the high scores we could get is turning in homework. So let's come up with a plan to up our average. We know doing some homework makes you learn better, so not doing any is not an option. But my plan hasn't been working. So, let's try this…"

Divide the class into teams of four.

Step One
STUDENT VOICE

Have students create two columns ~ one is GOOD Reasons FOR Doing Homework and column two is GOOD Reasons for NOT Doing Homework.

Step Two
STUDENT VOICE

Based on the information in the two columns and the two goals, devise a strategy for doing homework during this chapter/unit. Goal One would be for the homework to make a difference in their LEARNING not their grade. (In other words, it WILL make a difference in their grade but the strategy should be about the learning, not the grade.) The second goal would be to up the percentage of kids who turn in their homework. Be sure to have them be scanning the chapter itself for tips on how to make the strategy they devise applicable to this chapter/unit.

Step Three
STUDENT CHOICE

Either have them each apply their own strategy to their own group and have a competition or have them present their strategies to the class, and the whole class could then determine which strategy to use.

Step Four
ACTION RESEARCH

You will need to have the percentage of "turn in rates" for the past two-three units/time periods to share with them. You will also need their grade averages for each of the past two-three units. You can do this for each individual if you wish, however the "class" average needs to be the key measure. Set a whole-class goal for increasing the percentage of homework turned in and the percentage of grade increase for the whole class. (The extra bonus will be watching their own individual increases, but the idea is to begin thinking as a TEAM.)

Step Five
CELEBRATE

Maybe it will be a big celebration if they meet their class/team goal. Maybe it will be a "small victories" celebration if they didn't and you ask them why. Keep prodding. The more knowledge you can get from them, the more information you will have to devise a way that works. Competitions between classes? (NOT about highest averages but about MOST IMPROVED averages on both items.)

These five steps may take one, or even two periods. But, remember, they were skimming the chapter to devise their plan and ~ if it increases performance and compliance ~ it was time well-invested. If it doesn't work out quite as you wanted the first time, figure out ways to redesign this same approach and field test it in a different period.

INDIVIDUAL STRATEGY: 47-Minute Relationship Building

CLASSROOM STRATEGY FOR INDIVIDUALS

Spend a class period with an individual student ~ not the most difficult ~ but a kid who definitely needs to up his/her homework turn-in rates. Get a willing colleague to teach your class for one period. You have to plan this so that you don't leave class with the student, but intercept him/her so that other kids aren't asking where they're going.

Step One

This should be a "WHAT CAN I DO", not a "what can THEY do" meeting. Let them know you think the only thing stopping them from getting the grade they want is turning in homework. Tell them you have a goal for increasing their turn-in rate during this next chapter but need to find out from them how to do that.

Offer several possibilities:

1. Set a percentage of what they think they could get done (in other words you are telling them they can do one or two less in exchange for turning all the others in).

2. Come to an agreement on amount of each assignment this time (in other words, you are telling them they can do less problems in exchange for turning it in).

3. Ask for advice about what YOU could do to help them get it in.

4. Avoid at all costs the temptation to tell them what they are doing wrong.

5. Create other solutions as long as they are about how YOU are willing to make a change.

Step Two

Start working on tomorrow night's homework and give some one-on-one tutoring time. It should be the exact assignment you will hand out tomorrow. This kid will now have some of it done and feel some competence in their ability to do it and still know that even though it has 30 problems, he/she only has to finish 20.

Step Three

Leave some time to just chat. Have a topic in mind based on what you know about the kid: sports, interests, another teacher, school news/gossip. Just casual, upbeat conversation. Thank them for taking the time to talk to you.

Step Four

Be sure to notice and reinforce if they actually turn it in.

CAN YOU DO THIS FOR EVERY KID? OF COURSE NOT. DOES IT MAKE IT SEEM LIKE THEY'RE NOT AT FAULT? PERHAPS. IS IT FAIR TO OTHER STUDENTS? WORRY ABOUT ONE STUDENT AT A TIME. IF IT MAKES THIS KID FEEL BETTER ABOUT YOU AND YOUR CLASS… AND IF IT GETS HIM/HER TO BEGIN AT LEAST THINKING ABOUT TRYING HARDER, WON'T THAT MAKE YOU FEEL BETTER ABOUT THIS KID IN YOUR CLASS?

REFERENCES **Homework**

Blackstein, Alan M. "Failure is NOT an Option," Corwin Press, 2004.

Marzano, Pickering & Pollock. "Classroom Instruction that Works," ASCD 2001.

Science Daily. Stressing Competition May Drive Adolescents to Cheat in School, 1998.

Safe, Personalized Environments for Learning

Brain research is clear: Optimal learning occurs when the learner's emotional learning system is engaged so as to reinforce learning, not inhibit processing.

Emotion is a powerful vehicle to enhance memory, manage our demeanor, and increase creativity. Class climate and emotional safety are closely linked to a student's success.

"Teachers who nourish the emotional system serve as mentors for students by demonstrating sincere enthusiasm for their subject; by helping students discover a passion for learning; by guiding them toward reasonable personal goals and by supporting them in their efforts to become whatever they are capable of becoming."

Given, 2002

"Emotions, not cognitive stimulation, serve as the mind's primary architect for constructing its highest capacities: intelligence, morality, and sense of self."

Greenspan, 1997 (in Given)

REFERENCES

Safe, Personalized Environments for Learning

Given, Barbara. "Teaching to the Brain's Natural Learning Systems," ASCD, 2002.

Greenleaf, Robert. "Brain Based Teaching," Greenleaf & Papanek Publications, www.greenleaflearning.com, 2005.

Greenleaf, Robert & Wells-Papanek, Doris. "Memory, Recall, the Brain & Learning," Greenleaf & Papanek Publications, www.greenleaflearning.com, 2005.

McCombs, Barbara. "The Learner-Centered Framework on Teaching and Learning As a Foundation for Electronically Networked Communities and Cultures," http://pt3.org/technology/html/mccombs.html.

McCombs, Barbara & Whisler, Jo Sue. "The Learner-Centered Classroom and School," John Wiley & Sons, inc. 1997.

McTighe, Jay & O'Connor, Ken. "Seven Practices for Effective Learning," Educational Leadership, November 2005, V 63 no.3, p. 10.

Marzano, Robert J. "What Works in Schools," ASCD, 2003.

Marzano, Pickering and Pollock. "Classroom Instruction That Works," ASCD, 2001.

Student Voice, Motivation, & Aspirations

Voice "...student voice activities can create meaningful experiences for youth that help to meet fundamental developmental needs ~ especially for students who otherwise do not find meaning in their school experiences. Specifically, this research finds a marked consistency in the growth of agency, belonging and competence ~ three assets that are central to youth development."

Mitra, 2004

The Significance of Students: Can Increasing "Student Voice" in Schools Lead to Gains in Youth Development?

The notion of "student voice," or a student role in the decision-making and change efforts of schools, has emerged in the new millennium as a potential strategy for improving the success of school reform efforts. Yet few studies have examined this construct either theoretically or empirically. Grounded in a socio-cultural perspective, this article provides some of the first empirical data on youth participation in student voice efforts, by identifying how student voice opportunities appear to contribute to "youth development" outcomes in young people. The article finds that student voice activities can create meaningful experiences for youth that help to meet fundamental developmental needs ~ especially for students who otherwise do not find meaning in their school experiences. Specifically, this research finds a marked consistency in the growth of agency, belonging, and competence ~ three assets that are central to youth development. While these outcomes were consistent across the students in this study, the data demonstrate how the structure of student voice efforts and nature of adult/student relations fundamentally influence the forms of youth development outcomes that emerge.

Mitra, Teachers College Record ~ April 2004

Motivation ~ Research on learner efficacy stipulates that a learner needs to believe that they can, given reasonable effort, succeed at a task.

According to Jere Brophy (1987), motivation to learn is a competence acquired "through general experience but stimulated most directly through modeling, communication of expectations, and direct instruction or socialization by significant others (especially parents and teachers)."

"Intrinsic motivation refers to motivation to engage in an activity for its own sake. People who are intrinsically motivated work on tasks because they find them enjoyable."

Paul R Pintrich & Dale H. Schunk, *"Motivation in Education,"* **1995**

"Intrinsic motivation is the innate propensity to engage one's interests and exercise one's capacities, and, in doing so, to seek out and master optimal challenges."

John Marshall Reeve, *"Motivating Others,"* **1996**

"Intrinsic motivation is choosing to do an activity for no compelling reason, beyond the satisfaction derived from the activity itself ~ it's what motivates us to do something when we don't *have* to do anything."

James P Raffini, 1993

J. Condry and J. Chambers (1978) found that when students were confronted with complex intellectual tasks, those with an intrinsic orientation used more logical information-gathering and decision-making strategies than did students who were extrinsically oriented.

Students with an intrinsic orientation also tend to prefer tasks that are moderately challenging, whereas extrinsically oriented students gravitate toward tasks that are low in degree of difficulty. Extrinsically oriented students are inclined to put forth the minimal amount of effort necessary to get the maximal reward.

Lepper, 2003

Learner-Centered Principles Features

- "Practices integrate learning and motivational strategies to help students become <u>self-directed</u> learners;

- Instruction includes pre-assessments as well as ongoing assessments of students' interests, goals, background knowledge;

- Curriculum goals [that] are negotiated between all learners in the community;

- Student-designed assessment and feedback loops are present at the individual and group levels;

- Feedback is available for student … self-evaluation on progress;

- Feedback is available for others to see when students are 'ready' to submit work;

- Feedback provides ways for students to remediate and enrich their knowledge and skills in areas of choice, as appropriate;

- Concepts of 'emergent' curricula are at the heart of the system, wherein individual learners and the community of learners at any given period of time and based on their needs/purposes, can evolve and create curricula that include dynamic and up-to-date information;

- Flexibility and adaptability are central design features."

McCombs, 2005

Choice Theory® is the basis for all programs taught by the Institute. It states that all we do is behave, that almost all behavior is chosen, and that we are driven by our genes to satisfy five basic needs: *survival, love and belonging, power, freedom,* and *fun.* In practice, the most important need is *love and belonging,* as closeness and connectedness with the people we care about is a requisite for satisfying all of the needs.

Disconnectedness is the source of almost all human problems, such as what is called mental illness, drug addiction, violence, crime, school failure, spousal and child abuse, to mention a few. The 1998 book, **Choice Theory: A New Psychology of Personal Freedom,** is the primary text for all that is taught by the Institute.

Relationships and Our Habits

Seven Caring Habits	Seven Deadly Habits
Supporting	Criticizing
Encouraging	Blaming
Listening	Complaining
Accepting	Nagging
Trusting	Threatening
Respecting	Punishing
Negotiating differences	Bribing or rewarding to control

The William Glasser Institute

Aspirations

National Center for Student Aspirations: http://www.studentaspirations.org/

Dr. Russ Qualia

National Center for School Improvement: http://www.garyphillips.com/

Dr. Gary Phillips

REFERENCES

Achievement

Greenleaf and Wells-Papanek. "Memory, Recall, the Brain and Learning," www.greenleaflearning.com, 2005.

Marzano, Pickering & Pollock, "Classroom Instruction that Works," ASCD, 2001.

O'Shea, Mark R. "From Standards to Success," ASCD, 2005.

Reeves, Douglas B. "Accountability for Learning: How Teachers and School Leaders Can Take Charge," ASCD 2004.

Schmoker, Mike. "The Crayola Curriculum," Education Week, October 24, 2001.

Strong, Richard W. "Teaching What Matters Most: Standards and Strategies for Raising Student Achievement," ASCD, 2001.

Wolk, Ronald. Trivial Pursuits, Teacher Magazine, January 2003.

Coaching

Crane, Thomas G. "The Heart of Coaching: Using Transformation Coaching to Create a High Performance Culture," 2nd Edition. FTA Press, 2002.

Fried, Robert L. "The Game of School: Why We All Play It, How It Hurts Kids, and What It Will Take to Change It," Jossey-Bass, 2005.

Fried, Robert L. "The Passionate Teacher: A Practical Guide (2nd Edition)," Beacon Press, 2001. www.gse.harvard.edu.

Lewis, Michael. "Coach: Lessons on the Game of Life," W.W. Norton and Company, 2005.

Teaff, Grant. "Coaching in the Classroom: Teaching Self-Motivation," Cord Communications, 1994.

Whitmore, John. "Coaching for Performance: Growing People, Performance, and Purpose," 3rd Edition, Nicholas Brealey Publishing, 2002.

Wooden, John. "They Call Me Coach," McGraw-Hill Companies, Inc. 2004.

Motivation

Bell, Larry. Multicultural America, Inc. Workshop presentation, 2000.

Boynton, Mark and Boynton, Christine. "Preventing and Solving Discipline Problems," ASCD 2005.

Brophy, Jere. On Motivating Students. Occasional Paper No. 101. East Lansing, Michigan: Institute for Research on Teaching, Michigan State University, October 1986. 73 pages. ED 276 724.

Cotton, Kathleen. Northwest Regional Educational Laboratory, School Improvement Research Series. Close Up #7. www.nwrel.org. 2001.

Corbett, et. al. *Effort and Excellence in Urban Classrooms: Expecting ~ and Getting ~ Success with All Students,* Teacher's College Press, 2002.

Glasser, William. "Choice Theory in the Classroom," 1988, reprinted in Quill, 2001.

Glasser, William. Quality Teacher ~ as revised by Hammonds, Bruce, "The Leader-Teacher." www.leading-learning.co.nz.

Greenleaf, Robert K. "Creating and Changing Mindsets: Movies of the Mind," Greenleaf & Papanek Publications, www.greenleaflearning.com, 2005.

Kohn, Alfie. "Punished by Rewards," Educational Leadership, Sept. 1995.

Kohn, Alfie. "Unconditional Teaching," Educational Leadership, Sept. 2005.

Lepper, Mark R. "Motivational Considerations in the Study of Instruction," cognition and Instruction, 5, 4 (1988): 289-309.

McCombs, Barbara. "The Learner-Centered Framework on Teaching and Learning As a Foundation for Electronically Networked Communities and Cultures," http://pt3.org/technology/html/mccombs.html.

National Center for Student Aspirations, 5766 Shibles Hall, University of Maine, Orono, ME 04469, http://www.studentaspirations.org/research.htm.

National Research Council Institute of Medicine. "Engaging Schools: Fostering High School Students' Motivation to Learn," National Academies Press, 2004.

Raffini, James. "Winers Without Losers: Structures and Strategies for Increasing Student Motivation to Learn," Boston: Allyn and Bacon, 1993.

Reeves, John Marshall. *Motivating Others,* 1996.

Stipek, Deborah. "Motivation to Learn: From Theory to Practice, "Englewood Cliffs, New Jersey: Prentice Hall, 1988.

Phillips, Gary. National School Improvement Project, P.O. Box 11365, Bainbridge Island, WA. 98110.

Sagor, Richard. "Motivating Students and Teachers in an Era of Standards," ASCD, 2003.

Student Voice

Brooks, Jacqueline G. & Brooks, Martin G. "The Case for Constructivist Classrooms," Prentice Hall, 2001.

Cushman, Kathleen. "Fires in the Bathroom," New Press, 2003.

Fried, Robert L. "<u>The Passionate Learner: How Teachers and Parents Can Help Children Reclaim the Joy of Discovery</u>" Beacon Press, 2001.

Kohn, Alfie. "Unconditional Teaching," Educational Leadership, Sept. 2005, V 63 No.1.

McCombs, Barbara & Whisler, Jo Sue. "The Learner-Centered Classroom and School," John Wiley & Sons, inc.1997.

McCombs, Barbara. "Learner-Centered Principles and Technology," TeacherLine, January 2001.

McCombs, Barbara. "The Learner-Centered Framework on Teaching and Learning As a Foundation for Electronically Networked Communities and Cultures," http://pt3.org/technology/html/mccombs.html.

National Center for School Improvement. http://www.garyphillips.com/ ~ Dr. Gary Phillips.

National Center for Student Aspirations. http://www.studentaspirations.org/ ~ Dr. Russ Qualia.

Social Learning, Working Together, & Teamwork

Collaborative, interactive work is supported by the brain's Social Learning System.

Given, 2002

Cooperative Learning approaches have been shown to have an average +27% increase in academic achievement compared to when interactive student groupings are not used.

Marzano, Pickering & Pollock, 2001

Working WITH others is not the same as working AMONG others, at least not when it comes to engaging the brain fully. Barbara Given, in Teaching to the Brain's 5 Natural Learning Systems, demonstrates the need for learners to interact, to explore ideas and to communicate with others about their ideas. When students are considered a community of learners, they learn to build on the strength of working together to problem-solve, and to support each other in a constructive environment. Some key notions here are:

- The natural propensities of this system are the desires to belong to a group, to be respected, and to enjoy the attention of others.

- The tendency to associate, establish links, live side by side, and cooperate is an essential characteristic of humans. (Panksepp, 1998)

- Classroom and school norms take on extremely important roles regarding the development of socially acceptable behavior and in learning how to resolve conflicts. School needs to be a place where children get to know one another [as well as adults] at a deep level. (Given)

"Research has also shown that learning is enhanced in contexts where learners have supportive relationships, have a sense of ownership and control over the learning process, and can learn with and from each other in safe and trusting environments"

McCombs and Whisler, 1997

Teams ~ "Instructional improvement depends on.... simple data-driven formats - teams identifying and addressing areas of difficulty and then developing, critiquing, testing, and upgrading efforts in light of ongoing results."

Collins 01, Darling-Hammond 97, DuFour 02, Fullan 00, Reeves 00, Schaffer 88, Schmoker, 03, Senge 90, Wiggins 94

REFERENCES **Social Learning, Working Together, *&* Teamwork**

DuFour, Richard & DuFour, Rebecca. "On Common Ground: The Power of Professional Learning Communities," National Education Service, 2005.

DuFour, Richard & DuFour, Rebecca, Eaker, Robert & Karhanek, Gayle. "Whatever It Takes: How Professional Learning Communities Respond When Kids Don't Learn," National Education Service, 2004.

Given, Barbara. "Teaching to the Brain's Natural Learning Systems," ASCD, 2002.

Kagan, Spencer. Resources for Teachers, 1999

McCombs, Barbara & Whisler, Jo Sue. "The Learner-Centered Classroom and School," John Wiley & Sons, inc.1997.

Marzano, Pickering and Pollock. "Classroom Instruction that Works," ASCD 2001.

Schmoker, Mike. "Up and Away," Journal of Staff Development, Spring 2002.

Coaching Reluctant Learners **A Practical Framework for Classroom Success**

About the Authors

Billie Donegan

Billie Donegan is a national consultant on school reform, working with organizations including Brown University, Career Academy Support Network at UC Berkeley, and High Schools That Work. Billie has been a featured speaker at national and regional conferences in 17 states, including Alaska and Hawaii. A teacher at the high school and college level for over 31 years, she's received numerous teaching awards, including Texas Teacher of the Year for her work with minority high school students.

Billie developed the Keystone freshman success program and senior Capstone "next step" program that now serves as a national model, and is the author of three curriculum books and numerous professional articles. She received the NCAC 2002 Leadership award for her work with educational reform through smaller learning communities. Her work today primarily centers on whole school reform, successful transitions programs, and instructional practices for "coaching the reluctant learner."

With a Master's Degree in Communication from Colorado State University, Billie once again lives in the Rockies where she continues to write about students and work with teachers.

Contact Information:
billiedonegan@yahoo.com

Dr. Robert K. Greenleaf

Dr. Robert K. Greenleaf has served as a professional development specialist at Brown University. With experience in all grade levels K-16, he has 20 of years of service in public education ranging from Superintendent of Schools to Assistant Superintendent of Schools, District Coordinator of Student Aspirations, Elementary School Principal, Teacher, and Special Education Assistant. He has also taught at the College level.

President of Greenleaf Learning, founded in 1987, Bob specializes in educational strategies for understanding behaviors, building esteem and achievement, and brain-based learning for long-term memory and recall. Bob is the author of six instructional books, as well as many articles. He is the recipient of the "Outstanding Educator Award" from the Waterville Public Schools in Maine. Bob holds a Doctorate in Education from Vanderbilt University, a Masters in Educational Administration, and a Bachelor's degree in Psychology.

A past member of the National Speakers Association and Toastmasters International, he won several area and district speech events in the 1980's. His primary work is in the translation of research into practical applications for educators.

Contact Information:
www.greenleaflearning.com

Doris Wells-Papanek

Doris Wells-Papanek is a design consultant and learning coach. She applies brain-based research to design tailored learning tools for education and business. In education, she consults with and coaches students, teachers, faculty, administrators, and parents to empower learners to organize their time, tasks, and thoughts. In business, Doris works with designers, industry, and design schools to integrate users' mindsets and learning processes into sustainable product development.

As a partner of Greenleaf & Papanek Publications, Doris is the co-author of four brain-based instructional books. With over 25 years of experience in design, software, and education, Doris has developed corporate design strategies, managed user interface groups, taught design, researched and designed human-centered usability studies, and designed the appearance and behavior of software. She has worked with companies such as Xerox, Apple, Lotus, Hewlett-Packard, Siemens, Philips, and Intuit. Her work has led to over 20 design and utility patents.

Doris holds a Bachelors of Fine Arts in Product and Environmental Design from the Kansas City Art Institute and School of Design.

Contact Information:
www.tailoredlearningtools.com

BOOKS FOR SALE *Greenleaf & Papanek* **Publications**

COLLEGE EDITION
Stock ID: **ETS-C** Price: **$27**

GRADES 5-12 EDITION
Stock ID: **ETS-S** Price: **$27**

ENGAGING TODAY'S STUDENTS, What All Educators Need to Know *&* Be Able to Do

In these two editions of "Engaging Today's Students," we have examined the research around the learner of today, effective teaching practices, and the brain sciences that link to long-term memory and recall. We have observed hundreds of classroom lessons and activities, developed by an array of practicing educators. A strong indicator for how we organized this book was our deep commitment to learners ~ students as learners AND teachers as learners ~ and how we all can learn in significant and sustainable ways.

With a central focus on what today's learners require, we have created two editions, one with a focus on College level learners and the other referencing the needs of the grades 5-12 population of students. Each addresses the four essential learning components that drive student engagement.

Memory, Recall, the Brain *&* Learning

Explore ways of incorporating brain-based instruction in the classroom. The power of combining verbal and visual representations into powerful bi-modal memory packets. Over 40 teacher and student generated activities, organizers, templates, and strategies. Improve student performance!

Stock ID: **MRBL** Price: **$25**

Brain Based Teaching

Explore teaching and learning through three overarching lenses: How can I "frame" (design) the learning circumstance or activity to INVITE ALL learners, to participate? How can I design the learning experience to CAUSE learner processing ~ the work required for sustained learning and recall? How do I engineer tasks that create opportunities for multiple PATHWAYS (connections) to be formed for integration, application, & recall?

Stock ID: **BBT** Price: **$24**

Coaching Reluctant Learners

This book provides today's middle and high school teachers with the tools they need to ensure classroom success for today's students in a practical framework ~ unit-by-unit, where both teacher and student can feel more successful. Embedded in this book are proven strategies, activities, examples, and a framework for units that will improve student motivation and performance.

Stock ID: **CRL** Price: **$27**

A Mastery Toolkit

Speaking directly to the student, this book explores the foundations of understanding, essential strategies, and learning tools to become motivated, independently engaged in the learning process, responsible for learning, and accountable for making good choices. The goal is to become a "Can Do" Student ~ a student who takes charge of their learning and empowers themselves in ways to be successful.

Stock ID: **AMT** Price: **$25**

Creating *&* Changing Mindsets

If rational behavior was the basis for human interaction and the mysteries of learning and development were well understood ~ this book wouldn't be needed. Clear strategies to assist "shifts" in attitude and behavior are included. The question, "will this change last?" plagues us every year. Here's how to impact changes within a month's time... for long-term, sustained differences!

Stock ID: **CCM** Price: **$24**

Greenleaf & Papanek **Publications**
PO Box 186 Newfield, Maine 04056

BOOK ORDER FORM

Please mail this form, to the above address,
with a check, or

Fax a Purchase Order to:
fax   847.615.9958

bob@greenleaflearning.com
tel   207.793.8675

doris@tailoredlearningtools.com
tel   847.615.9957

NAME	
CO/ORG/SCHOOL	
ADDRESS	
CITY	
STATE/ZIP CODE	
EMAIL	
TELEPHONE	
CHECK or PO #	
DATE	

Make checks payable to **GREENLEAF LEARNING**.

For more information, please visit our websites:
www.greenleaflearning.com
www.tailoredlearningtools.com

For Discounts on Bulk Orders Over 10 Books Total: Call 207.793.8675

INSTRUCTIONS	DISCOUNT CALCULATOR

1 Enter the "Quantity" of each book you are buying
2 Add the total number of books and multiply by the "discount" amount using the "Discount Calculator"
3 Multiply "Quantity" x "Price" and enter the amounts due for each book in the "Totals" column
4 Add the extended total in the "Subtotal" box
5 Subtract the quantity discount and then add shipping fees to arrive to your final "TOTAL COST."

2 books total	=	**$1** discount per book
3 books total	=	**$2** discount per book
4 books total	=	**$3** discount per book
5-10 books total	=	**$4** discount per book

STOCK ID	QUANTITY	PRICE	TOTALS
ETS-C college		x $27	=
ETS-S grades 5-12		x $27	=
MRBL		x $25	=
BBT		x $24	=
CRL		x $27	=
AMT		x $25	=
CCM		x $24	=
discount	x =	subtotal	=
		less discount	-
		total	=
		shipping 1-4 books	+ $3.50
	additional shipping for more than 4 books add .50 cents each		+
		Canada add $3.00	+
		TOTAL COST	=